ISLAMIC STUDIES

BOOK: 2

INTERMEDIATE LEVEL (GRADE EIGHT)

by

Dr. Abu Ameenah Bilal Philips

ISBN 1 898649 18 9

British Library Cataloguing in Publication Data.

A catalogue record for this book is available from the British Library.

First Edition, 1416 AH/1996 CE

Cover design: Abu Yahya

Typeset by: Al-Hidaayah Publishing and Distribution

Published by: Al-Hidaayah Publishing and Distribution
              P.O. Box 3332
              Birmingham
              United Kingdom
              B10 9AW

              Tel: 0121 753 1889
              Fax: 0121 753 2422
              E-Mail: AHPD@HIDAAYAH.DEMON.CO

CONTENTS

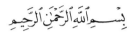

FOREWORD

Al-Madinah Islamic School was founded in Los Angeles in the year 1979 with the goal of protecting the cultural identity of Muslim children in that area. This goal was formulated in an attempt to meet some of the crushing needs of Muslims in America for their own educational institutions. It had become clearly evident by the 1970s that the greatest crisis facing Muslims in America was the loss of the younger generations. Muslim communities across the country were generally unable to successfully transfer Islaam to their children. The destructive environment of government junior and senior high schools throughout America continues to de-Islamicise the vast majority of Muslim children to this day.

The only way to stem the tide was to develop alternative means of education wherein the social and spiritual environment of the students could be carefully monitored and Islamically directed. Weekend Islamic schools as well as evening classes in masjids and Islamic Centers were started from the sixties, but their effect was minimal. Four or five hours a week of Islamic teaching in the evenings or on weekends cannot hope to successfully compete with thirty hours of secular education and socialization. The only realistic solution was full-time Islamic schools, staffed and run by Muslims. Al-Madinah school is one such attempt. A number of schools were started around the country in the seventies and eighties, but the majority have folded after a few years of operation due, in most cases, to financial problems.

Al-Madinah Islamic School goes from kindergarten to the eighth grade and was plagued from its inception with the problem of the lack of materials and curriculums for Islamic Studies in English. During the early eighties, the school directors became acquainted with Brother Abu Ameenah Bilal Philips, who was then teaching Islamic Studies at the Manaret al-Riyadh Islamic School in Saudi Arabia. With his excellent Islamic background as a graduate of Islamic Studies from the Islamic University of Madeenah, he was able to develop materials and a curriculum for Islamic Studies on the secondary level. *Alhamdulillaah*, at

7

our request Brother Bilal made these materials available to us and since then we have been using them in a modified form to suit our particular needs at Al-Madinah Islamic School.

We at Al-Madinah School were quite happy to see the publication of *Islamic Studies: Book 1* in 1990, which has effectively presented Islamic educational material for grade seven, and we felt honored to be invited to introduce Book 2 in the series. *Islamic Studies: Book 2* continues to present the subjects of *Tawheed, Tafseer, Hadeeth* and *Fiqh* in very simple language, yet with appropriate depth based on thoroughly researched and authenticated material. The curriculum in the preface is very useful for educational institutions. The questions at the end of each chapter are well thought out and convenient for both teachers and students. The book is a welcome addition to the field of Islamic Studies for English-medium Islamic schools and among the best available on the market, without a doubt. It is our hope that the remaining books in the series will be available soon and that they will also enjoy the success and popularity which Book 1 has met and which we are certain Book 2 will meet, Allaah willing.

The staff of Al-Madinah Islamic School and the Los Angeles community which it serves heartily thank Dr. Abu Ameenah Bilal Philips for his efforts and ask Allaah to bless him and guide him in the service of Islaam and Muslims.

Eric 'Ali, M.A. Education
Director
Al-Madinah Islamic School
Los Angeles, California, U.S.A.

28 September 1993.

PREFACE

This text is based on the Islamic Studies syllabus covering the following four major areas of study: *Tawheed, Tafseer, Hadeeth* and *Fiqh*. It is therefore assumed that the "Qur'aanic skills" of reading and recitation would be covered in Arabic classes, and "Islamic History" including the *Seerah* (Biography of the Prophet [☀]) would be included either in the Social Studies syllabus as a major topic, or taught as a separate subject.

Aims of the Course

1. To acquaint the student with the uniqueness of the Islamic concept of God and how it affects man's relationship with God, with his fellow man and with the creation in which he lives. This may be achieved through the study of *Tawheed* (Islamic Monotheism).

2. To introduce the student to the meanings of the final book of revelation, the Qur'aan, and their relevance to daily life, as opposed to the ritual recitation of the Qur'aanic text without any realization of its meanings whatsoever. This could be developed during the study of *Tafseers* (commentaries) of the *Soorahs* (Qur'aanic chapters).

3. To familiarize the student with his Islamic rights and obligations and present a clear and authentic picture of how they may be fulfilled. This would best be accomplished in the detailed study of *Fiqh* (Islamic Law) and *Tawheed*.

4. To develop in the student a realization that Islaam is built on firm, clear, logical principles and that it is not merely a collection of irrelevant cultural practices handed down from earlier generations. This can be done through the study of the sciences (*Usool*) of *Hadeeth* (Prophetic traditions), *Fiqh* and *Tafseer*.

5. To identify and build an Islamic character in the student through the study of Islaamic ethics which is, no doubt, an essential component of any Islaamic Education curriculum. This field of study

9

is to be found in the Prophetic traditions (*Hadeeth*), which have been carefully chosen for in-depth study and discussion at all levels.

Method of Presentation

The order in which the topics have been arranged is based on the aims and their priority. *Tawheed* represents the most fundamental principle of Islaam, while the teachings of Islaam are based on the Qur'aan (the understanding of which is called *Tafseer*), and the *Sunnah* (the teachings of the Prophet (ﷺ) contained in *Hadeeths*). This application of the teachings falls within the framework of *Fiqh* (Islamic Law). The teacher, however, is free to vary the order according to the class response and his or her personal preference, as long as the whole syllabus is covered.

Arabic terminology should be used and properly pronounced wherever possible, and students should be held responsible for understanding the important transliterated terms mentioned in the text. Terms written in Arabic script should not be emphasized unless the whole class is able to read and write Arabic in script. Accordingly, the teacher's treatment of Arabic terms should take into account the fact that in any given grade, there may be students who are raw beginners in Arabic. In this way, the teacher may avoid double penalization of a student whereby a poor mark in Arabic automatically results in a poor mark in Islamic Education.

Discussion about each of the topics of the syllabus should be encouraged among the students and reasoned explanations should be given to their questions where possible. Ample time should be also be allotted at the end of each class for general questions, as Islaamic Education covers all aspects of human life and the Islaamic Studies teacher will also be required to fulfill the role of counsellor or student advisor. The Islaamic Studies teacher should attempt to find answers to all the students' questions by making personal research using advanced reference materials and by contacting outstanding Islaamic scholars in their region. The student may also be given wider individual or group term research projects on the topics to further stimulate discussion and interest.

At the end of Book 1 (Grade 7) there is a selected bibliography of available English reference works used in the preparation of this series, as well as works which may be used by both teachers and students to obtain further information on the topics covered.

Division of Lessons

The material covered by the four major topics represents a full school year's work; therefore, the sub-topics have been distributed over two semesters according to a timetable allotting two to three lessons per week for Islaamic Studies. Consequently, three weeks have been given to each topic for study, review and testing. Questions are given at the end of each sub-topic as homework, which should be reviewed before beginning the next sub-topic. A general review of the material of the sub-topics may be given at the end of the third week, followed by a test. If time constraints develop, wherein in becomes necessary to omit a part of the syllabus, it is advisable to aim at exposure to all of the major topics and confine syllabus reduction to the number of _Hadeeths_ and/or _Soorahs_ (chapters of the Qur'aan covered in _Tafseer_) prescribed for daily study. The following is a sample work scheme which has been used at Manarat Al-Riyadh Schools, with some variation, for nearly ten years.

Sample Work Scheme

Grade 9: First Term

TOPIC	SUB-TOPIC	WEEK
TAWHEED	Charms and Omens	1-2
	Review and Test	3
TAFSEER	Usool at-Tafseer:	
	The Seven Recitations	4
	Tafseer of Soorah al-Inshiraah	5
	Review and Test	6

Grade 9: Second Term

Content

A concerted effort has been made to ensure that all of the material contained in this series of texts in authentic. This is of the utmost importance where the dissemination of Islaamic knowledge is concerned. It has been the practice in books of this type, especially those prepared for children, to take great liberties in presentation. However, this should not be the case, because it is from such simple incorrect beginnings that major deviations may fester and grow. The *Hadeeths* mentioned in the texts have also been referenced to English translations of *Hadeeth* classics which are currently available in order to facilitate further research for English speakers. This job was largely undertaken by brother Iftekhar Mackeen, to whom I am indeed grateful. In the case of *Fiqh* issues, I have not preferred any particular school of thought (*Mathhab*), but have instead endeavored to follow the school which has the strongest support in the Qur'aan and *Sunnah*.

It should also be noted that, although this series of texts was originally designed for the teaching of Islaamic Studies in English junior and senior high school levels, it has also been prepared with new Muslim reverts in mind. Consequently, it is quite suited for courses in Islaam for English speaking adults. In fact, I have personally used them for a number of lecture series delivered to both Muslim reverts and Muslims by birth.

May Allaah accept these efforts to spread the knowledge of Islaam on an institutional level and bring it to fruition, as success lies ultimately in His hands alone.

Abu Ameenah Bilal Philips
Riyadh, Saudi Arabia.
1993/1414 A.H.

TRANSLITERATION

In order to provide the non-Arab with a more easily read set of symbols than those in current use, I have adopted a somewhat innovative system of transliteration, particularly with regard to long vowels. It should be noted, however, that a very similar system was used by E.W. Lane in preparing his famous *Arabic-English Lexicon*, which is considered the most authoritative work in its field. There are many other similar scholarly text written systems, for example, Margaret K. Omar's *Saudi Arabic: Urban Hijazi Dialect* (Washington DC: Foreign Service Institute, 1975), as well as the Foreign Language Institute's *Saudi Arabic: Headstart* (Monetery, CA: Defense Language Institute, 1980).

No transliteration can express exactly the vocalic differences between two languages, nor can Roman characters give anything more than an approximate sound of the original Arabic words and phrases. There is also the difficulty of romanizing certain combinations of Arabic words which are pronounced differently from the written characters. Included in this category is the prefix *"al"* (representing the article "the") when it precedes words beginning with the letters known as *al-Huroof ash-Shamseeyah.* (lit. "the solar letters"). The sound of "l" is merged into the following letter; for example, *al-Rahmaan* is pronounced *ar-Rahmaan*. In the case of all other letters, known as *al-Huroof al-Qamareeya* (lit." the lunar letters"), the "al" in pronounced fully. I have followed the pronunciation for the facility of the average reader to writing *ar-Rahmaan* instead of *al-Rahmaan,* and so on.

Consonants

	a		ا ٰ	aa
٬	u		و ٫	oo
ٖ	i		ي ٖ	ee

Consonants

ء	'		ض	**d**
ب	b		ط	**t**
ت	t		ظ	**th**
ث	th		ع	'
ج	j		غ	gh
ح	**h**		ف	f
خ	kh		ق	q
د	d		ك	k
ذ	**th**		ل	l
ر	r		م	m
ز	z		ن	n
س	s		ه	h
ش	sh		و	w
ص	**s**		ي	y

Shaddah (ّ): The *Shaddah* is represented in Roman letters by doubled consonants. However, in actual pronunciation, the letters should be merged and held briefly like the "*n*" sound produced in the *n/kn* combination in the word *unknown*, or the "*n*" in *unnerve*, the "*b*" in *grabbag*, the "*t*" in *freight-train*, the "*r*" in *overruled*, the "*p*" in *lamp post*, and the "*d*" in *midday*.

1. TAWHEED: THE CATEGORIES OF SHIRK

Tawheed cannot be completely understood unless its opposite, *Shirk*, is also carefully studied. The sin of *Shirk* denies the very purpose of man's creation, and is to Allaah the greatest of sins:

$$ إِنَّ ٱللَّهَ لَا يَغْفِرُ أَن يُشْرَكَ بِهِۦ وَيَغْفِرُ مَادُونَ ذَٰلِكَ لِمَن يَشَآءُ $$

"Surely Allaah will not forgive the association of partners (*Shirk*) with Him, but He forgives (sins) less than that of whomever He wishes."

Soorah an-Nisaa' (4) : 48

Shirk literally means partnership, sharing or associating, but Islamically it refers to assigning partners to Allaah in whatever form it may take. For one's *Tawheed* to be correct and pure, all forms of *Shirk* must be erased from one's beliefs and practices. This is why the declaration of faith consists of two parts: One negates false gods and *Shirk*, and the other confirms the uniqueness of Allaah. *Laa ilaaha* denies that anyone or anything deserves worship, and *il-lal-laah* restricts worship to Allaah alone. Together they complete the declaration of belief in *Tawheed*.

The following analysis of *Shirk* is according to the three broad categories developed in the study of *Tawheed* in Book 1. We will first look at the main ways in which *Shirk* can occur in the area of *Ruboobeeyah* (Lordship), then *al-Asmaa' was-Sifaat* (Divine Names and Attributes), and finally in *'Ebaadah* (Worship).

SHIRK IN TAWHEED AR-RUBOOBEEYAH

This category of *Shirk* includes both the belief that others share Allaah's control and rule over the creation, as well as the belief that there exists no Lord over the creation at all. Thus, this form of *Shirk* may be divided into two main categories:

(A) Shirk by Association:

This is the form of Shirk in which people believe in most of God's qualities and powers, but they believe that God has parts. God is recognized as the creator and sustainer of the universe and His powers and knowledge are believed to be limitless, but He Himself is considered to be divisible.

For example, though most Christians say they believe in One God, they also say He is Trinity. They say He is made up of three units, all separate, yet supposedly equal: God the father, God the son and God the Holy Spirit.[1]

Hindus also believe in One God called Brahman, but they, too, believe that He takes three forms: Brahma the creator-god, Vishnu the preserver-god and Shiva the destroyer-god.[2]

According to *Tawheed*, God is one in all senses. He is a special One which cannot be divided like the ones in His creation. He is a perfect One and nothing can be one like Him.

Another example of this type of *Shirk* which occurs today is that of those who pray to the dead. They believe that the souls of righteous humans can continue to affect the affairs of this world, even after their deaths. Their souls, it is believed, can fulfill human needs, remove calamities and aid whoever calls on them. Therefore, grave worshippers give human souls the divine ability to cause or change events in this life, which in fact only Allaah can do. This belief of theirs means that others share Allaah's rule over creation. The correct Islamic belief is that the dead have no power to affect the lives of the living. Prophet Muḥammad (ﷺ) was reported to have said, "*When a man dies, his acts come to an end, except in the case of three: an ongoing charity, beneficial knowledge, or a pious child who prays for him.*"

---

[1] *Dictionary of Religions*, p.337.
[2] W.L. Reese, *Dictionary of Philosophy and Religion* (New Jersey: Humanities Press, 1980), pp.66-67 and 586-587.

(B) Shirk by Negation:

In this form of *Shirk*, Allaah's existence is completely denied. An ancient example is that of the Pharaoh of Prophet Moses' time. God mentioned in the Qur'aan that he negated the existence of God and claimed to Moses and the people of Egypt that he, Pharaoh, was the only true lord of all creation. God quoted him as saying to Moses, **"If you choose a god besides me, I will surely imprison you"**[3] and to the people he proclaimed, **"I am your Lord, the Most High."**[4]

Another example of this form of Shirk is the belief of some philosophers that the world is eternal, without beginning or end. They attempt to escape the questions surrounding the beginning to escape the questions surrounding the beginning of man's creation and that of the universe by claiming that there was none. To support this claim, they invented theories which gave Allaah's attributes of being without beginning and end to matter which He has created. Present-day holders of this belief are the communists, as well as some scientists who claim that matter has no beginning and everything is a product of matter, including the human mind and life itself.

SHIRK IN TAWHEED AL-ASMAA' WAS-SIFAAT

This category of *Shirk* includes both the belief that God is like a man and the belief that man is like God. This form can also be subdivided into two categories with regard to in the area of God's names and attributes:

(A) Shirk by Humanization:

In this form of *Shirk*, God is given the form and qualities of human beings. Paintings or statues are made of Him in which He is given the shape of a man. The Hindus and Buddhists worship idols in the likeness of men and call them God. Similarly, many Christian churches

---

[3] Soorah ash-Shooraa (26) : 29.
[4] Soorah an-Nazi'aat (79) : 24.

have pictures and statues of a human being, Jesus Christ, which they claim represents God. Because they believe that God looks like a man, they also attributed to Him human weaknesses. In the Bible it is claimed that God took a rest after spending six days to create the world.[5] Elsewhere God is spoken of as repenting for His bad thoughts as humans do when they realize their errors.[6] However, in the Qur'aan, Allaah teaches man that He is unlike anything:

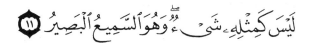

"There is nothing like Him, yet He hears and sees all things."

Soorah ash-Shooraa (42) : 11

(B) Shirk by Deification:

This form of *Shirk* happens when created beings or things are given Allaah's names or attributes. It was the practice of the ancient Arabs to worship idols whose names were derived from the names of Allaah. Their three main idols were *al-Laat,* taken from Allaah's name *al-Elaah; al-'Uzza,* taken from *al-'Azeez;* and *al-Manaat,* taken from *al-Mannaan.* There was also in the area of Arabia called Yamaamah a false prophet who took the name *Rahmaan,* which only belongs to Allaah.

Einstein's Theory of Relativity ($E = mc^2$, energy is equal to mass times the square of the speed of light) taught in all schools is in fact an expression of *Shirk* in *al-Asmaa' was-Sifaat.* The theory states that energy can neither be created nor destroyed, it merely transforms into matter and vice versa. However, both matter and energy are created entities and they both will be destroyed, as Allaah clearly states:

---

[5] Genesis 2:2, "And on the seventh day God finished his work which he had done and he rested on the seventh day from all his work which He had done." (*Holy Bible,* Revised Standard Version [Nelson, 1951], p.2).

[6] Exodus 32:14, "And the Lord repented of the evil which he thought to do to his people." (*Holy Bible,* R.S.V. [Nelson, 1951]).

"Allaah is the Creator of all things...."

Soorah az-Zumar (39) : 62

كُلُّ مَنْ عَلَيْهَا فَانٍ

"Everything in the world will perish...."

Soorah ar-Rahmaan (55) : 26

The theory also implies that mass and energy are eternal, having no beginning or end, since they are supposed to be uncreated and transform into each other. However, this attribute belongs only to Allaah, Who alone is without beginning or end.

The Christian belief that Prophet 'Eesaa (Jesus) was God can also be considered *Shirk* by deification. Jesus was a man and a prophet of Allaah. His birth without a father was miraculous, but so was Eve's birth without a mother and Aadam's birth without a father or a mother.

SHIRK IN TAWHEED AL-'EBAADAH

This category of *Shirk* refers to the act of worshipping others along with Allaah. In this category, worship which belongs only to Allaah is shared with others. Like the other categories, it can also be divided into two major sections:

(A) Ash-Shirk Al-Akbar (Major Shirk):

When any form of worship is performed for others besides Allaah, it is the form known as "ash-Shirk al-Akbar" (Major Shirk). It represents the most obvious form of idolatry which the prophets were specifically sent by Allaah to call the masses of mankind away from and to establish *Tawheed al-'Ebaadah* in its place. Allaah's stated this in the Qur'aan as follows:

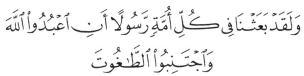

"Surely we have sent to every nation a messenger saying, "Worship Allaah and avoid Taaghoot (false gods)."

Soorah an-Nahl (16) : 36

Taaqhoot actually means anything which is worshipped along with Allaah or instead of Allaah. For example, love, in its perfection, is a form of worship which should only be directed to Allaah. In Islaam, the love of Allaah is expressed by total obedience to Him. The kind of love which is worship is not the type of love which man naturally feels towards creation, such as parents, children, food, etc. To direct that natural type of love towards Allaah is to lower Him to the level of His creation, which is *Shirk* in *al-Asmaa' was-Sifaat*. Love which is worship is the total surrender of one's will. Consequently, Allaah told the Prophet (ﷺ) to tell the believers,

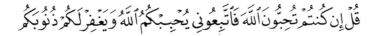

"Say: If you love Allaah, follow me and Allaah will love you."

Soorah Aal-'Imraan (3) : 31

The Prophet (ﷺ) also told his companions, *"None of you is a true believer until I become more beloved to him than his child, his father and the whole of mankind."*[7] Love of the Prophet (ﷺ) is not based on his humanity, but on the divine origin of his message. Thus, like the love of Allaah, it is also expressed by total obedience to his commands. Allaah said in the Qur'aan,

مَن يُطِعِ ٱلرَّسُولَ فَقَدْ أَطَاعَ ٱللَّهَ

"Whoever obeys the Messenger obeys Allaah"

Soorah an-Nisaa' (4) : 80

and

قُلْ أَطِيعُوا۟ ٱللَّهَ وَٱلرَّسُولَ

---

[7] Reported by Anas and collected by al-Bukhaaree (*Sahih al-Bukhari* (Arabic-English), vol.1, p.20, no.13) and Muslim (*Sahih Muslim* (English Trans.), vol.1, p.31, no.71).

"Say: Obey Allaah and obey the Prophet..."

Soorah Aal-'Imraan (3) : 32

If man allows anything or anyone to come between himself and Allaah, then he has worshipped that thing. In this way, money can become one's god, or even one's desires could become a god. The Prophet (ﷺ) said, *"The worshipper of the Dirham will always be miserable."*[8] Allaah said in the Qur'aan,

أَرَءَيۡتَ مَنِ ٱتَّخَذَ إِلَـٰهَهُۥ هَوَىٰهُ

"Have you not seen the one who takes his desires as his god?"

Soorah al-Furqaan (25) : 43

The reason why so much emphasis has been placed on *Shirk* in 'Ebaadah (worship) is because it contradicts the very purpose of creation as expressed in Allaah's statement:

"I have not created the *Jinn* and mankind except for My worship."

Soorah ath-Thariyaat (51) : 56

This form of *Shirk* represents the greatest act of rebellion against the Lord of the Universe and is thus the ultimate sin. It is a sin so great that it virtually cancels out all good a person may do and guarantees him a place in the Hell-fire.

(B) Ash-Shirk Al-Asghar (Minor Shirk):

Mahmood ibn Lubayd reported that Allaah's Messenger (ﷺ) said, *"The thing I fear for you the most is **ash-Shirk al-Asghar (Minor Shirk)**." The companions asked, "O Messenger of Allaah, what is Minor **Shirk**?"*

---

[8] Collected by al-Bukhaaree (*Sahih al-Bukhari (English-Arabic)*, vol.8, p.296, no.443).

*He replied, "**ar-Riyaa**" (showing off), for verily Allaah will say on the Day of Resurrection when people are receiving their rewards, 'Go to those for whom you were showing off in the material world and see if you can find any reward from them.*"[9]

Riyaa' is the practice of performing any of the various forms of worship in order to be seen and praised by people. This sin destroys all the benefits that lie in righteous deeds and brings on the one who commits it a severe punishment.

It is a part of human nature to love leadership and praise. Doing religious acts to impress people in order to be praised by them is therefore a most fearful evil. This danger becomes really significant to Muslims since their goal is to make all of the acts of their lives acts of worship. In fact, the likelihood that true believers would commit *ash-Shirk al-Akbar* is small, since its pitfalls are so obvious. But, for the true Believer, the chance of committing *Riyaa*' is great because it is so hidden. Ibn "Abbaas alluded to this fact when he said, "**Shirk** *in the Muslim nation is more hidden than a black ant creeping on a black stone in the middle of a moonless night.*"[10] It only involves the simple act of changing one's intention. Also, the motivating forces behind it are very strong since it comes from man's inner nature.

Thus, great care has to be taken to ensure that one's intentions begin pure and remain pure whenever righteous deeds are being done. This is why the saying of Allaah's name has been enjoined before all acts of importance. A series of *Du'aas*[11] have also been prescribed before and after all natural habits like eating, drinking, sleeping, and even going to the toilet, in order to turn these everyday habits into acts of worship and develop in the Muslim a keen awareness of Allaah. It is this awareness, called *Taqwaa*, which ensures that intentions remain pure.

---

[9] Collected by Aḥmad, aṭ-Ṭabaranee and al-Bayhaqee in *az-Zuhd*. See *Tayseer al-'Azeez al-Ḥameed*, p.118.
[10] Reported by Ibn Abee Ḥaatim and quoted in *Tayseer al-'Azeez al-Ḥameed*, p.587.
[11] Informal prayers.

The Prophet (ﷺ) also provided protection against the inevitable acts of *Shirk* by teaching certain specific prayers which may be said anytime. Abu Moosaa said, *"One day Allaah's Messenger delivered a sermon saying, 'O people, fear **Shirk**, for it is more hidden than the creeping of an ant.' Those whom Allaah wished asked, 'And how do we avoid it when it is more hidden than the creeping of an ant, O Messenger of Allaah ?' He replied, 'Say.*

> *(Allaahumma innaa na'oothu bika an nushrika bika shay'an na'lamuh, wa nastaghfiruka limaa laa na'lamuh).*
>
> O Allaah, we seek refuge in you from knowingly committing Shirk with you, and we ask your forgiveness for what we do not know about.'"[12]

---

[12] Collected by Ahmad and at-Tabaraanee.

QUESTIONS

1. The term *Shirk* in Islaam means
   (a) to disbelieve.
   (b) to take a partner.
   (c) to believe in the oneness of Allaah.
   (d) to give Allaah a partner in any way.
   (e) to believe that Allaah has no partner of any kind.

2. *Shirk* may take place in *Tawheed ar-Ruboobeeyah* in one of the following two ways:
   (a) by denying Allaah's existence and by making Him like created beings as the Christians do when they worship images of God.
   (b) by giving Allaah a partner and by praying to idols as the Hindus do.
   (c) by believing that the dead can affect the affairs of this world and by praying to saints as some Muslims do.
   (d) by believing that there is more than one God and by offering prayers to be seen by others as hypocrites do.
   (e) by giving Allaah a partner and by denying His existence as the Communists do.

3. The belief that matter can neither be created nor destroyed is
   (a) *Shirk* in *Tawheed ar-Ruboobeeyah* because it makes Allaah like creation.
   (b) *Shirk* in *Tawheed al-Asmaa' was -Sifaat* because it gives Allaah's attributes to created things.
   (c) *Shirk* in *Tawheed al-'Ebaadah* because it denies the Creator's existence.
   (d) *Shirk* in *Tawheed al-Asmaa' was-Sifaat* because only Allaah deserves to be worshipped.
   (e) *Shirk* in *Tawheed ar-Ruboobeeyah* because it denies the creation of matter.

4. Directing prayer to Prophet Muhammad (ﷺ) is a form of *Shirk* in

    (a) Tawheed al-Asmaa' was-Sifaat because it denies creation's existence.

    (b) Tawheed al-'Ebaadah because it assigns a partner to mankind.

    (c) Tawheed al-'Ebaadah because prayer should only be directed towards Allaah.

    (d) Tawheed al-Asmaa' was -Sifaat because it gives Allaah man's qualities.

    (e) Tawheed al-'Ebaadah because it involves making man like God.

5. Those who claim that 'Alee was God in person or claim that Jesus was God commit

    (a) Shirk in *Tawheed al-Asmaa' was-Sifaat* by giving Allaah attributes of the Creator.

    (b) Shirk in *Tawheed ar-Ruboobeeyah* by giving man the qualities of creation.

    (c) Shirk in *Tawheed al-'Ebaadah* by giving creation the attributes of the Creator.

    (d) Shirk in *Tawheed al-'Ebaadah* by denying the existence of creation.

    (e) Shirk in *Tawheed al-Asmaa' was-Sifaat* by giving man the qualities of God.

6. Drawing, painting or carving images of God is a form of

    (a) Shirk in *Tawheed al-Asmaa' was-Sifaat* because it makes Allaah like His creation.

    (b) Shirk in *Tawheed al-'Ebaadah* because it makes the Creator like what He created.

    (c) Shirk in *Tawheed al- ar-Ruboobeeyah* because it denies Allaah's existence altogether.

    (d) Tawheed al-Asmaa' was-Sifaat because it gives God the attributes of the Creator.

    (e) Shirk in *Tawheed ar-Ruboobeeyah* because it gives Allaah a partner.

7. Minor (hidden) *Shirk* is to be feared most because

    (a) it is a part of human nature to worship, and hidden *Shirk* only involves the simple act of changing one's intention from doing a religious act for people to doing it to be seen by Allaah.

    (b) it is natural to change one's intention and everyone loves to admire the Creator. Therefore, it is easy to do minor *Shirk* by doing religious acts for the pleasure of God.

    (c) everyone naturally loves to be admired, and minor *Shirk* is produced by the simple process of changing one's intention from doing worship for Allaah to doing it to be admired by people.

    (d) human nature is such that it hates praise and loves to be ignored. Thus, man easily falls into minor *Shirk* because it is merely doing religious acts to be praised by Allaah instead of doing them for God.

    (e) the act of changing one's intention is very easy, and it is part of human nature to praise God. Hence, falling into minor *Shirk* is easy since it only involves changing one's intention from worship for Allaah's pleasure to worship in order to be praised by God.

8. Write out the *Du'aa* for seeking refuge from hidden *Shirk* and its meaning in English.

2. TAWHEED: 'ULOO (HIGHNESS)

Allaah, Most Great and Glorious, has described Himself in order that man may have a better understanding of who He is. Since the human mind is limited in its knowledge and scope, it is impossible for it to understand something which has no limits. Therefore, Allaah, Most Merciful, took it upon Himself to reveal to man some of His attributes in order that man may not confuse the attributes of created things with those of Allaah.

Among Allaah's attributes is the attribute of *al'Uloo*, or highness. When used to describe Allaah, this attribute refers to the fact that Allaah is above His creation. He is neither enclosed by His creation nor is any part of creation above Him in any way.

Significance

This attribute has special significance to man, who prior to the arrival of Islaam in its final form had strayed far away from the meaning of this noble attribute. Christians had claimed that Allaah came to earth in the form of a man, that is, that Allaah had become a part of His Creation. The Jews before them also claimed that Allaah came down to earth in the form of a man and wrestled with Prophet Ya'qoob.[13] The Persians regarded their kings as gods and worshipped them directly, while the Hindus believed that Brahman, the main god, was in every place and in everything, so they worshipped countless idols, animals and human beings.

The idea that Allaah is everywhere also became a part of Christian belief and eventually found its way among Muslims many generations after the Prophet's time. This idea became so widespread that if one were to ask most Muslims today the question, "Where is Allaah?", they would immediately reply that He is everywhere.

---

[13] Genesis 32 : 24-30.

The Danger of the "Everywhere" Belief

The main danger of this belief is that it encourages the worship of created things. If one believes that God is everywhere, it means that He is present inside His creation. People who hold this belief are likely to worship God through His creation because it is easier to worship a god who can be seen than one who is invisible. This type of belief commonly leads to the worship of human beings, for, if Allaah is everywhere, people like to think of Him as being more in humans than in animals, plants or rocks because humans are superior to the other forms of creation. Once this idea is accepted, the door has been opened for someone to claim that Allaah is more in him than anyone else. And, anyone who accepts this claim automatically begins to worship him. Thus, the Pharaohs of Egypt and the Chosroes of Persia were worshipped as gods, and Prophet 'Eesaa (Jesus) became a god for Christians.

CLEAR PROOFS

There are a number of proofs which could be used to establish the fact that Allaah is totally separate from and above His creation. The following are five such proofs:

1.   A Natural Proof:

Man, from the Islamic viewpoint, is born with certain natural tendencies and is not just the product of his environment. This fact is based on the Qur'anic passage in which Allaah explained that when He created Aadam, He extracted from him all of his descendants and made them bear witness to His Unity.[14] This concept is further emphasized by the Prophet's statement, *"Every child which is born but has the natural inclination (Fitrah) to worship Allaah, but its parents turn it into a Jew or a Christian."*[15] If Allaah is everywhere and exists in everything, it would mean that He could be found in filth and filthy places. When

---

[14]   Soorah al-A'raaf (7) : 172.

[15]   Reported by Abu Hurayrah and collected by al-Bukhaaree (*Sahih al-Bukhari* (Arabic-English), vol.8, pp.389-390, no.597) and Muslim (*Sahih Muslim* (English Trans.), vol.4, p.1399, no.6429.

confronted with this conclusion, most people naturally reject it. They find themselves instinctually unable to accept any statement which implies that Allaah, Creator of the universe, is present in man's excrements or in any other items or places not befitting His majesty. Therefore, since man's natural instincts, placed in him by Allaah, reject the claim that Allaah is everywhere, it is highly unlikely that such a claim would be correct.

2. The Prayer Proof:

According to the rules and regulations governing prayer in Islaam, places of worship must be completely free from statues or pictures that represent Allaah or His creation, and the various positions of worship used in _Salaah_ (bowing, prostrating, etc.) are prohibited from being directed to anyone or anything besides Allaah. If Allaah were present everywhere and in every individual, it would be perfectly acceptable for people to worship each other or even worship themselves. Similarly, it would be allowable for people to worship stones, trees, animals and even idols, but Islaam forbids all of this. Islaam came to take man away from the worship of man and other created beings, and lead them to the worship of the Creator alone. It is totally prohibited for man to perform prayer to created things and beings under any circumstance. This Islamic prohibition proves that Allaah is not to be found within His creation.

3. The Mi'raaj Proof:

Two years before his migration to Madeenah, the Prophet (ﷺ) made a miraculous night journey (_Israa'_) from Makkah to Jerusalem, and from Jerusalem he took the _Mi'raaj_ up through the seven skies in order to be in the direct presence of Allaah. It was there, above the seventh heaven, that _Salaah_ was made compulsory five times per day, Allaah spoke directly to the Prophet (ﷺ) and He revealed to him the last verses of _Soorah al-Baqarah_.[16] If Allaah were everywhere, there would have been

---

[16] See _Sahih al-Bukhari_ (Arabic- English), vol.9, pp.449-450, no. 608 and _Sahih Muslim_ (English Trans.), vol.1, pp. 103-104, no.313 for the Prophet's account of this incident.

no need for the Prophet (ﷺ) to go anywhere. He could have been in the direct presence of Allaah on earth in his own house. Therefore, the *Mi'raaj* is itself proof that Allaah is above His creation and not a part of it.

4. The Qur'anic Proof:

There are many verses in the Qur'aan which directly or indirectly state that Allaah is above His creation. They are found in almost every chapter of the Qur'aan. For example, in *Soorah* al-Ikhlaas, Allaah calls Himself *as-Samad,* which means that to which things rise. This can be understood literally, as in the case of the angels about whom Allaah said,

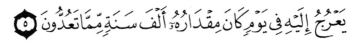

"They ascend up to Him in a day whose length is like a thousand years by your reckoning."

Soorah as-Sajdah (32) : 5

It can also be understood spiritually, as in the case of *Du'aa* and *Thikr,* about which Allaah said,

"Every good saying goes up to Him."

Soorah Faatir (35) : 10

Allaah also calls Himself al-'Alee, which means the highest, above which there is nothing, for example, *"Al-'Alee al-Kabeer."*[17] He also referred to Himself as being above His servants saying.

وَهُوَٱلْقَاهِرُفَوْقَعِبَادِهِۦ

"He is *al-Qaahir* (the Irresistible) above His worshippers."

Soorah al-An'aam (6) : 18, 61

---

[17] Soorah Sabaa (34) : 23

He also described His worshippers as,

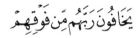

"Those who fear their Lord Who is above them."

Soorah an-Nahl (16) : 50

Therefore, the Qur'aan itself clearly points out for those who think deeply about its meanings, that Allaah is high above His creation and not within it or surrounded by it in any way.[18]

5. The Proof from the Sunnah:

There is also evidence from the statements of the Prophet (ﷺ) which clearly establishes that Allaah is not on the earth or within His creation.

Mu'aawiyah ibn al-Hakm said, "I had a servant girl who used to tend to my sheep in the area of Mount Uhud at a place called al-Jawwaameeyah. One day I came to see them only to find that a wolf had made off with a sheep from her flock. Although I am from Aadam's descendants who regrets like the rest, I gave her face a terrible slap. When I came to Allaah's Messenger (ﷺ) with the story, he considered it a grave thing for me to have done, so I said, 'O Messenger of Allaah, couldn't I free her?' He said, 'Bring her to me.' So, I brought her. He asked her, 'Where is Allaah?' and she replied, 'Above the sky.' Then he asked her, 'who am I?' and she replied, 'You are Allaah's Messenger.' So he said, 'Free her, for verily she is a believer.'"[19]

If Allaah were everywhere, the Prophet (ﷺ) would have had to correct her statement, "Above the sky," since whatever was said in front of him which he did not disapprove of is considered "approved *Sunnah.*" The Prophet (ﷺ) not only accepted her statement, but he also used it as a basis for judging her to be a true believer.

---

[18] *al-'Aqeedah at-Tahaaweeyah*, pp.285-286.

[19] Collected by Muslim (*Sahih Muslim* (English Trans.), vol.1, pp.271,272, no.1094).

Summary

It can be said that according to the Islamic principles of *Tawheed*:

1. Allaah is completely separate from His creation.
2. Creation neither surrounds Him, nor is it above Him in any way.
3. He, Allaah, is above all things.

This, however, does not deny Allaah's awareness of all that happens in the Universe, since His knowledge is everywhere and His vision catches all things. In fact, Allaah is so aware that He knew the minute details of all that would happen in every corner of the universe before He even created it. This is what is meant by the verses,

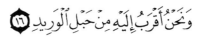

"And we are closer to him than his jugular vein."

Soorah Qaaf (50) : 16

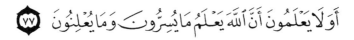

"Be aware that Allaah comes between a man and his heart."

Soorah al-Anfaal (8) : 24

These verses should not be taken to mean that Allaah is inside man at a point closer than his jugular vein or that He is inside man's heart changing its states. They simply imply that nothing escapes Allaah's knowledge, even the innermost thoughts of man, and nothing is beyond His power to control and change, even the emotions of the heart. Allaah said,

"Don't they realize that Allaah knows what they hide and what they expose?"

Soorah al-Baqarah (2) : 77

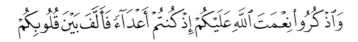

"(Remember) when you were enemies and He put love between your hearts and by His blessings you became brothers."

Soorah Aal-'Imraan (3) : 103

The Prophet (ﷺ) often used to pray saying,

(Yaa mugallib al-Quloob, thabbit qalbee 'alaa deenik.) "O Changer or hearts, steady my heart on Your religion." [20]

Therefore, according to the classical Islamic outlook based on the Qur'aan and the Sunnah of the Prophet (ﷺ), Allaah is above the universe and its contents in a way which befits His majesty and He is not in any way contained within His creation nor is it within Him, but His infinite knowledge, mercy and power operate on every particle within it without any hindrance whatsoever.[21]

---

[20] Collected by at-Tirmithee and authenticated by Muhammad Naasirud-Deen al-Albaanee in *Saheeh Sunan at-Tirmithee*, vol.3, p.171, no.2792.

[21] 'Umar al-Ashqar, *al-'Aqeedah fee Allaah* (Kuwait: Maktabah al-Falaah, 2d ed., 1979), p.171.

QUESTIONS

1. The main danger of the "everywhere" belief is that
    (a) it may lead to the worship of created things.
    (b) it causes man to make images of Allaah's throne.
    (c) it causes us to believe that Allaah is above His creation.
    (d) it leads to the worship of the Prophet (ﷺ), because he performed miracles.
    (e) it causes man to believe himself greater than God.

2. Proof by human nature that Allaah is above His creation is
    (a) if Allaah could be found everywhere, then worshipping idols would not be considered Haraam.
    (b) Allaah said in the Qur'aan that He is above His creation.
    (c) Allaah's name al-'Alee means that He is above all things.
    (d) if Allaah is everywhere, the Prophet (ﷺ), would not have gone out of the universe in the Mi'raaj to be in Allaah's presence.
    (e) believing that Allaah is everywhere means that He is in filthy places, and such a belief is rejected by all young children.

3. Proof that Allaah is not surrounded by His creation according to the prayer proof is
    (a) if Allaah was surrounded by His creation, He would be found in our feces, which is a thought naturally rejected by the masses of the people.
    (b) that it is allowable to worship Allaah without seeing Him.
    (c) if Allaah's creation surrounded Him, He could not possibly be above His creation as He described Himself in the Qur'aan.
    (d) if Allaah were surrounded by His creation, worshipping idols, humans and other created things would not have been made forbidden in Islaam.
    (e) none of the above.

4. Allaah described Himself
    (a) because man needs to know what Allaah looks like.
    (b) because Allaah is without limits and man's limited mind cannot understand the infinite.
    (c) because Allaah did not want man to disbelieve in Him.
    (d) because Allaah did not want man to confuse the religion of Islaam with the religion of earlier prophet.
    (e) because the human mind can only picture Allaah if it is given a correct picture by Allaah.

5. The attribute al-'Uloo in reference to Allaah
    (a) means that Allaah is greater than His creation.
    (b) means that creation surrounds Allaah.
    (c) refers to Allaah's presence in all parts of creation.
    (d) means that Allaah is above His creation, yet enclosed by it.
    (e) refers to the fact that Allaah is not enclosed by His creation and that He is above his creation.

6. Christian, Jewish, Hindu and Persian beliefs concerning the attribute al-'Uloo is that
    (a) they all believe that God exists within His creation.
    (b) they all made idols in which they claimed Allaah was living.
    (c) they all called certain human beings Allaah, or God, and worshipped them.
    (d) they all considered God to be made up of different parts.
    (e) most of them believed that God died on earth. ·

7. Proof that Allaah is completely separate from His creation according to the Prophet's statement (_Hadeeth_) is
    (a) the prophet (ﷺ) said to Mu'aawiyah ibn al-Hakam that he should free his slave girl because she said that he (the Prophet) was the Messenger of Allaah.
    (b) Mu'aawiyah said that Allaah was above the heavens.
    (c) the Prophet (ﷺ) said to Mu'aawiyah, _"Free your slave girl because she is a true believer."_
    (d) when the Prophet (ﷺ) asked Mu'aawiyah's slave girl where Allaah was, she replied, _"Above the heavens."_
    (e) during the Mi'raaj, the Prophet (ﷺ) said that he did not see Allaah, but that he saw only light

8. Although Allaah is above the universe

(a) He does not know everything which is going on in the universe.

(b) He knows everything which goes on in the universe, but He cannot see everything.

(c) His knowledge is everywhere except in dirty places.

(d) He knows all, sees all, and nothing happens without His permission.

(e) He knows all and sees all, but bad things happen against His will and without His permission

9. When Allaah said in the Qur'aan, "**I am closer to man than his jugular vein**" and "**I come in between a man and his heart**," it means that

(a) Allaah controls man completely by being inside his body.

(b) Allaah is inside man whenever he thinks and whenever He wants him to do things.

(c) Allaah is inside man, but not the rest of creation.

(d) Allaah is everywhere, including dirty places.

(e) Allaah has knowledge of man's inner thoughts and can change his heart as He wishes.

3. TAWHEED: SEEING ALLAAH IN THIS LIFE

Allaah's Image

As was said previously, man's mind is limited and Allaah is limitless, therefore man cannot understand anything about Allaah's attributes except what Allaah chooses to reveal to him. If man tries to picture Allaah in his mind, he will only go astray because Allaah is different from anything man can think of. Whatever man imagines is from some part of creation, or a combination of some created things which he has observed. For example, gremlins, unicorns, vampires, ninja turtles, supermen, transformers, etc. are all imaginary figures made up of existing beings or objects. Thus, if man pictures Allaah in his mind, he ends up giving Allaah the attributes of creation.

It is, however, possible for man to understand some of Allaah's attributes, for example *al-Qaadir* (the All-Powerful). This means that there is nothing which Allaah is unable to do. Similarly, *ar-Rahmaan* (the Most Merciful), means that there is nothing in creation which has not been blessed by Allaah's mercy. This understanding does not require any mental pictures. Thus, it is only along these lines that the human mind may think about Allaah. Confusion in this area is one of the ways in which Christians went astray from the true teachings of God. They put in their churches and shrines pictures and statues of Allaah in the form of an old European man with a big white beard. One of the main reasons why they went astray this way is because they depended on the distorted Torah of the Jews for religious guidance. In the first book of the Torah, called Genesis, the Jews had written the following concerning man's creation:

> "Then God said, 'Let us make a man in our image, after our likeness... so God created man in his own image, in the image of God He created him."[22]

---

[22] Genesis 1:26, 27.

From these verses and others like them, Christians concluded that Allaah looks like a man and thus they represented Him that way in their statues and paintings. But in the Qur'aan, Allaah makes it very clear that nothing we can think of is like Him. Allaah states,

$$\text{لَيْسَ كَمِثْلِهِ شَيْءٌ وَهُوَ السَّمِيعُ الْبَصِيرُ ﴿١١﴾}$$

"There is nothing like Him, but He sees and hears all."

Soorah ash-Shooraa (42) : 11

$$\text{وَلَمْ يَكُن لَّهُ كُفُوًا أَحَدٌ ﴿٤﴾}$$

"There is none comparable to Him."

Soorah al-Ikhlaa<u>s</u> (112) : 4

PROPHET MOOSAA (ﷺ) ASKS TO SEE ALLAAH

After making it clear that He is not like His creation, Allaah goes on to inform us that our eyes cannot see Him. He said,

$$\text{لَّا تُدْرِكُهُ الْأَبْصَارُ وَهُوَ يُدْرِكُ الْأَبْصَارَ}$$

"Eyes cannot catch Him but He catches all eyes."

Soorah al-An'aam (6) : 103.

In order to emphasize this fact to us, Allaah tells us in the Qur'aan the following story of Prophet Moosaa[23]:

$$\text{وَلَمَّا جَاءَ مُوسَىٰ لِمِيقَاتِنَا وَكَلَّمَهُ}$$
$$\text{رَبُّهُ قَالَ رَبِّ أَرِنِي أَنظُرْ إِلَيْكَ قَالَ لَن تَرَانِي وَلَٰكِنِ انظُرْ}$$
$$\text{إِلَى الْجَبَلِ فَإِنِ اسْتَقَرَّ مَكَانَهُ فَسَوْفَ تَرَانِي فَلَمَّا تَجَلَّىٰ}$$
$$\text{رَبُّهُ لِلْجَبَلِ جَعَلَهُ دَكًّا وَخَرَّ مُوسَىٰ صَعِقًا فَلَمَّا أَفَاقَ}$$
$$\text{قَالَ سُبْحَانَكَ تُبْتُ إِلَيْكَ وَأَنَا أَوَّلُ الْمُؤْمِنِينَ ﴿١٤٣﴾}$$

---

[23] Moses.

"And when Moses came to our appointed meeting place and his Lord spoke to him, he said, "My Lord! Show yourself so that I may gaze upon you.' He replied, 'You will never see Me, but look at the mountain. If it remains in its place you will be able to see Me.' When his Lord revealed all His glory to the mountain, it was crushed into dust, and Moses fell down unconscious. When he regained his consciousness he said, "Glory be unto you! I turn to you repentant and I am the first among the true believers."

Soorah al-Aa'raaf (7) : 143

Prophet Moosaa thought that he might be allowed to see Allaah since Allaah had favoured him over the rest of mankind of that time, by choosing him to receive His message and favoured him over the other prophets by continually communicating with him directly. But Allaah made it very clear to him that it just was not possible. Moosaa could not bear the intensity of even seeing Allaah's glory, much less Allaah's boundless being.[24] Prophet Moosaa at once realized his error and begged Allaah's forgiveness for requesting something which was out of place.

DID PROPHET MUHAMMAD (ﷺ) SEE ALLAAH?

Some people have thought that an exception was made in the case of the last of the Prophets, Muhammad (ﷺ), to whom Allaah caused to travel up through the heavens and go even beyond the point where Angels were allowed to go. But, when 'Aa'eshah was asked by one of the *Taabi'oon,* [25] Masrooq, if Prophet Muhammad (ﷺ) saw his Lord, she replied, " *My hair is standing on end because of what you have asked! Whoever tells you that Muhammad saw his Lord has lied!*"[26] Abu Tharr asked the Prophet (ﷺ) if he saw his Lord. The Prophet (ﷺ) replied, *"There was only light, how could I see Him?"*[27] The Prophet

---

[24]   *al-'Aqeedah at-Tahaaweeyah,* p. 191.

[25]   Students of the Prophet's companions.

[26]   Collected by Muslim (*Sahih Muslim* (English Trans.), vol.1, pp.111-112, no.337 and 339).

[27]   Collected by Muslim (*Sahih Muslim* (English Trans.), vol.1, p.113, no.341.

(ﷺ) on another occasion explained the significance of the light and that it was not Allaah Himself, saying, *"Verily Allaah doesn't sleep nor is it befitting for Him to sleep. He is the One who lowers the scales and raises them. The deeds of the night go up to Him before the deeds of the day and those of the day before those of the night, and **His veil is light**."*[28]

Thus, it can safely be said that the Prophet (ﷺ), like the Prophets before him, did not see Allaah, Most Great and Glorious, in this life. Likewise, the claim of those who are supposed to have seen Allaah in this life is also proven false. If the prophets (ﷺ), whom Allaah preferred over all of mankind, were unable to see Allaah, how could any man, no matter how religious and pious he may be, see Allaah? Such a claim implies that the one who makes it is greater than the prophets, God forbid.

SHAYTAAN PRETENDS TO BE ALLAAH

There is no doubt that many of those who claim to have seen Allaah saw something. They saw visions of light and possibly even unearthly beings. But, the fact that many of them often drop basic practices of Islaam after such visions clearly shows that what they are involved with is satanic and not divine. They often claim that they do not need to regularly make *Salaah* or *Sawm* as common people because they have risen spiritually above the level of the masses. Sheikh 'Abdul-Qaadir al-Jeelaanee (1077-1166) gave an account of an incident which he once experienced. This incident contains an explanation for both the visions of those who claim to have seen Allaah, as well as the reason why they often discard basic Islamic practices after such visions. "One day," he said, " I was deeply involved in worship when all of a sudden I saw before me a grand throne with a brilliantly shining light surrounding it. A thunderous voice then struck my ears, 'O 'Abdul-Qaadir, I am your Lord! For you I have made lawful that which I have forbidden for other.' 'Abdul-Qaadir asked, 'Are you Allaah besides whom there is no god?' O enemy of Allaah.'" And with that the light vanished and darkness blanketed him. The voice then said, "'Abdul-Qaadir, you have succeeded

---

[28]   Reported by Abu Moosaa al-Ash'aree and collected by Muslim (*Sahih Muslim* (English Trans.), vol.1, p.113, no.343).

in beating my trap because of your understanding of the religion and your knowledge. I have managed to misguide over seventy saintly worshippers by such incidents." Afterwards, the people asked 'Abdul-Qaadir how he realized Satan by his claim that Allaah had made lawful for him that which He had forbidden for others. He knew that the divine law revealed to the Prophet (ﷺ) could not be canceled or changed. He also realized who it was when Shaytaan announced that he was the Lord, but was unable to confirm that he was Allaah, who is without partner.[29]

Similarly, some people in the past have reported that they have seen the *Ka'bah* and circled it in visions. Others have reported seeing a great throne stretched out before them with a glorious being seated on it and a large number of men ascending and descending around it. They considered the men to be angels and the glorious being to be Allaah, the Exalted and Glorious, but in fact, it was Satan and his followers.[30]

Thus, the basis of the claims to have seen Allaah, either in dreams or in broad daylight, can be traced back to Satanic psychological and emotional states. In these states, Satan takes on glorious light forms and claims to those who are experiencing the vision that he is their Lord. Due to their ignorance of pure *Tawheed*, they accept such claims and thereby go astray.

THE MEANING OF SOORAH AN-NAJM

Some people[31] mistakenly thought that the following verses meant that the Prophet (ﷺ) saw Allaah when he was on the uppermost horizon:

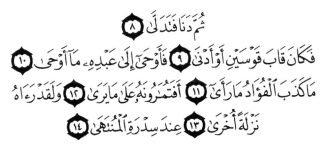

---

29 Ibn Taymeeyah, *at-Tawassul wal-Waseelah* (Riyadh: Dar al-Iftaa, 1984), p.28.
30 Ibid.
31 Among them is an-Nawaawee in his commentary on <u>Saheeh</u> Muslim called *Sharh <u>Saheeh</u> Muslim*.

"Then he came close and descended until he was two bow's lengths away or closer. And He revealed to His slave that which He revealed. The heart did not lie about what it saw. Will you argue with him about what he saw? And verily he saw him yet another time. By the lote-tree of the uppermost boundary."

Soorah an-Najm (53) : 7-14

It is claimed that the above verses were in reference to the Prophet (ﷺ) seeing Allaah, but when someone asked the Prophet's wife 'Aa'eshah about these verses, she replied, " I was the first person from this *Ummah* to ask the the Messenger of Allaah about them and he replied, *'Verily it was Jibreel, may Allaah's peace be on him. I never saw him in the form in which he was created except these two times: I saw him descending from the heavens and the greatness of his size filled all that was between the sky and the earth.''* 'Aa'eshah then said, "Haven't you heard that Allaah, Most High, said,

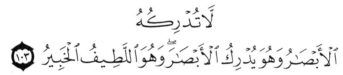

'Eyes can't catch Him, but He catches all eyes and He is the Subtle, the Aware'[32]?'

"And, haven't you heard that Allaah said,

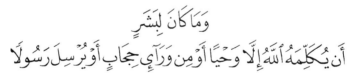

"Allaah will not speak to any man except by inspiration, or from behind a veil, or by sending a messenger (angel)."[33],[34]

---

[32] Soorah al-An'aam (6) : 103.

[33] Soorah ash-Shooraa (42) : 51.

[34] Collected by Muslim (*Sahih Muslim* (English Trans.). vol.1, pp.111-112, no.337.

[35] Reported by Abu Hurayrah and collected by al-Bukhaaree (*Sahih al-Bukhari* (Arabic-English), vol.9, pp.390,391, no.532) and Muslim (*Sahih Muslim* (English Trans.), vol.1p.115, no.349).

If Allaah could be seen in life, the tests of this life would not have any meaning. What makes this life a real test is the fact that we must believe in Allaah without actually seeing Him. If Allaah were visible to us, everyone would believe in Him and in all that the Prophet (ﷺ) taught. In fact, man would end up like the angels, in total obedience to Allaah. However, Allaah made man to be higher than the Angels, whose belief in Allaah is without choice. Therefore, man's choice of belief over disbelief had to be in a situation where Allaah's existence could be questioned. Thus, Allaah has kept Himself hidden from mankind and will continue to do so until the Last Day.

SEEING ALLAAH IN THE NEXT LIFE

There are many instances in the Qur'aan where Allaah has stated plainly that we will see Him in the next life. In describing some of the events on the Day of Resurrection Allaah says,

"On that day some faces will be bright, looking at their Lord."

Soorah al-Qiyaamah (75) : 22-23

The Prophet (ﷺ) has explained even more about this great event. When asked by some of his companions, *"Will we see our Lord on the Day of Resurrection?"* He replied, *"Are you harmed by looking at the moon when it is full?"* They replied, *"No."* He then said, *"Verily you will see Him likewise."*[35] On another occasion he said, *"Verily each one of you will see Allaah on the day when you must meet Him, and there will not be between Him and you a veil nor a translator."*[36] Ibn 'Umar also reported that once the Prophet (ﷺ) said, *"The Day of Resurrection is the first day that any eye will look at Allaah, Most Great and Glorious."*[37] Seeing Allaah is a special added blessing for the people of Para-

---

[36] Reported by 'Adee ibn Abee Haatim and collected by al-Bukhaaree (*Sahih al-Bukhari* (Arabic-English), vol.9, p.403, no.535).

[37] An authentic *Hadeeth* collected by ad-Daaraqutnee and ad-Daarimee in his book *ar-Radd 'alaa al-Jahmeeyah* [Refutation of the Jahmites] (Beirut: al-Maktab al-Islaamee, n.d.), p.57.

dise. This additional favor is greater than all the other pleasures which Allaah has saved for the righteous inheritors of the garden. Allaah refers to this additional pleasure saying,

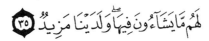

"For them is whatever they wish and there is with Us something additional."

Soorah Qaaf (50) : 35

Two of the Prophet's most notable companions, 'Alee ibn Abee Taalib and Anas were reported to have explained that the additional thing which Allaah referred to here is looking at Him.[38] The companion Suhayb reported that Allaah's Messenger (ﷺ) recited (the verse):

"For those who do right is a good reward and (something) additional",[39] and said, *"When the people deserving Paradise have entered it and those deserving Hell have entered it, a crier will call out, 'O people of Paradise, Allaah has a promise for you which He wished to fulfill.' They will ask, 'What is it ? Has He not made our scale (of good deeds) heavy, made our faces shining, put us in Paradise and extracted (some of) us from Hell ? The veil will then be removed and they will gaze at Him. Nothing which He has bestowed on them will be more dear to them than gazing at Him. And that is the something additional."*[40]

As for the previously mentioned verse, **"Eyes cannot catch Him, but he catches all eyes,"** it negates seeing Allaah in this life, but in the next life, it only negates the possibility of seeing Allaah in His totality. The righteous will only be able to see a part of Allaah since their sight will still be the sight of finite created beings, while Allaah is and always will be the infinite uncreated Lord who cannot be encompassed by sight, knowledge or power.[41] As for the disbelievers, they will not see Allaah

---

[38] Collected by at-Tabaree (*al-'Aqeedah at-Tahaaweeyah*, p.190).

[39] Soorah Qaaf (50) : 35.

[40] Collected by at-Tirmithee, Ibn Maajah and Ahmad.

[41] *al-'Aqeedah at-Tahaaweeyah*, p. 188, 193, 198. See also Soorah Taahaa (20) : 110 where Allaah says, **"They (man) cannot encompass Him with (their) knowledge."**

in the next life, which will be a great deprivation and disappointment for them. Allaah said,

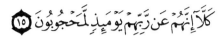

"But on that day they will be veiled from their Lord."
Soorah al-Mutaffifeen (83) : 15

SEEING PROPHET MUHAMMAD (ﷺ)

Many people have claimed to have seen the Prophet (ﷺ) and to have received special guidance from him. Some claim that their visions were in dreams, while others claim to have actually seen him while they were awake. Those who make such claims are usually highly honored by common people. They often introduce a variety of religious innovations and attribute them to the Prophet (ﷺ). The basis of these claims rests on the *Hadeeth* (authentic) reported by Abu Hurayrah, Abu Qataadah and Jaabir ibn 'Abdullaah in which the Prophet (ﷺ) said, *"He who saw me in a dream in fact saw me, for Satan cannot assume my form."*[42] This *Hadeeth* is *Saheeh* and reliable and thus cannot be denied or distrusted. However, there are some points which should be noted concerning its meaning:

(a) The *Hadeeth* confirms that fact that Satan can come in dreams in various forms and invite man to misguidance.
(b) The *Hadeeth* states that Satan cannot take the form or appearance of the prophet (ﷺ).
(c) The *Hadeeth* also confirms the fact that the Prophet's form may be seen in dreams.

Since the Prophet (ﷺ) made this statement about dreams to his companions, who were familiar with his appearance, it means that if one who knows **exactly what the Prophet (ﷺ) looks like** sees someone fitting that description in a dream, he could be sure that Allaah has

---

[42] Collected by al-Bukhaaree (*Sahih al-Bukhari* (Arabic-English), vol.9. p.104, no.123) and Muslim (*Sahih Muslim* (English Trans.), vol.4, p.1225, no.5635 and p.1226, no.5639).

blessed him with a vision of the Prophet (ﷺ). That is because Allaah has prohibited Shaytaan from taking the actual form of the Prophet (ﷺ). However, this also means that Shaytaan can appear in dreams to those unfamiliar with the Prophet's appearance and claim to be Allaah's Messenger. He may then prescribe religious innovations for the dreamer or inform him that he is *al-Mahdi*, the awaited reformer, or even Prophet 'Eesaa, who is to return in the last days. The number of individuals who have started innovations or made such claims based on dreams are countless. People are particularly inclined to accept such claims because of their misunderstanding of the various implications of the *Hadeeth*. Since the *Sharee'ah* is complete the claim that the Prophet (ﷺ) has come in dreams with new additions must be false. Such a claim implies one of two things: (1) Either that the Prophet (ﷺ) did not fulfill his mission in his lifetime, or (2) that Allaah was not aware of the future of the *Ummah* and thus did not prescribe the necessary in junctions during the Prophet's lifetime. Both of these meanings contradict basic principles of Islaam and thus, any such claim is totally unacceptable.

As for seeing the Prophet (ﷺ) while awake, such a claim goes beyond the boundaries of the *Hadeeth* into the impossible. Any such vision which actually occurs would no doubt be the work of Shaytaan, regardless of the outcome. During the Prophet's miraculous night journey to Jerusalem and into the heavens, Allaah did miraculously show him a number of the former prophets, and Prophet Muhammad (ﷺ) communicated with them. Those who claim to see Prophet Muhammad (ﷺ) while they were awake, in fact, attempt to elevate themselves to his level. Any such innovations in the religion of Islaam, whether based on visions of the Prophet (ﷺ) or otherwise, are totally unacceptable based on the many statements of the Prophet (ﷺ) prohibiting them, such as 'Aa'eshah's report that the Prophet (ﷺ) said, "*Whoever innovates in this affair of ours (i.e. Islaam) something not belonging to it, will have it rejected.*"[43]

---

[43]　Collected by al-Bukhaaree (*Sahih al-Bukhari* (Arabic-English), vol 3, p.535, no.861), Muslim (*Sahih Muslim* (English Trans.), vol.3, p.931, no.4266) and Aboo Daawood (*Sunan Abu Dawud* (English Trans.), vol.3, p.1294, no.4589.

QUESTIONS

1. Man cannot understand anything about Allaah except what Allaah tells him because
   (a) man's mind is limitless and Allaah is limited.
   (b) Allaah has no limits and neither has man's mind.
   (c) man is a creation of Allaah's mind, which is limited.
   (d) Allaah is limitless and man's mind is limited.
   (e) Allaah has set no limits on what man can understand.

2. Humans go astray when they try to picture Allaah in their minds because.
   (a) whatever man thinks of is only a picture of Allaah and not really Allaah.
   (b) man's mind cannot picture something with many limits.
   (c) Allaah is different from anything that man can imagine.
   (d) man can only imagine things which really exist.
   (e) whatever man imagines will only be a small part of Allaah.

3. Christians went astray concerning Allaah's image because
   (a) they depended on Hindu scriptures, which described Allaah in human terms.
   (b) they did not follow the Jewish scriptures.
   (c) Prophet Jesus told them to worship him as God.
   (d) God showed himself to them in the form of a man.
   (e) none of the above.

4. Prophet Moosaa thought that he might see Allaah in this life because
   (a) God had preferred him over the rest to creation at that time.
   (b) Allaah had promised him that he would see Him.
   (c) he had many followers who had already seen Allaah.
   (d) the prophets before him had seen Allaah.
   (e) Allaah used to appear to him in the form of a burning bush.

5. The significance of the story about Prophet Moosaa asking to see Allaah is that
    (a) all of mankind will be able to see Allaah in this life.
    (b) only the prophets will be able to see Allaah.
    (c) Prophet Moosaa was the only prophet not allowed to see Allaah.
    (d) man is not able to see Allaah in this life.
    (e) some prophets were not allowed to see Allaah.

6. The claim that one has seen Allaah is false
    (a) because only the prophets were allowed to see Allaah.
    (b) since one who claims that makes himself greater than God.
    (c) because such a claim would make one greater than the prophets, who only saw God in their dreams.
    (d) as it makes Allaah like created things and the prophets greater than Allaah.
    (e) since it makes one greater than the prophets, who were not allowed to see Allaah.

7. The wisdom behind not seeing Allaah in this life is that
    (a) to do so would make the tests of this life pointless.
    (b) it teaches man patience in life and in death.
    (c) man's mind is boundless and Allaah in limitless.
    (d) to see Him is to give Him the characteristics of created things.
    (e) many who claim to have seen Allaah usually drop basic practices of Islaam.

8. The Qur'aanic proof that man will see Allaah is
    (a) in the Prophet's statement *"There was light and I could see him!"*
    (b) found in the verse, **"Eyes cannot catch Him, but He catches all eyes."**
    (c) that Prophet Moosaa asked to see Allaah and was granted his wish.
    (d) in Allaah's statement, **"Allaah surrounds all things."**
    (e) none of the above.

9. Allaah will be seen
    (a) on the Day of Judgement by all men, women and children.
    (b) in the dreams of the prophets, martyrs and the righteous.
    (c) on earth just before the end of the world.
    (d) in the next life by the righteous believers in God.
    (e) on the Day of Resurrection by the most evil of mankind.

10. The Qur'anic verse, "**Eyes cannot catch Him, but He catches all eyes**," means that
    (a) man will never be able to see Allaah.
    (b) only the believers will be able to see Allaah in this life.
    (c) Allaah sees only things which human beings see.
    (d) Allaah is invisible.
    (e) Allaah is not visible to man in this life.

11. Proof that Prophet Muhammad (ﷺ) did not see Allaah can be found in

    (a) 'Aa'eshah's statement "*Verily it was I who saw Allaah, Muhammad only saw Jibreel!*"
    (b) the Prophet's statement, "*Surely I have seen Allaah in the uppermost heavens, but you will not see Him before the Day of Judgement.*"
    (c) Abu Tharr's report that when he asked the Prophet (ﷺ) if he had seen his Lord, he replied, *"There was only light, how could I see Him?"*
    (d) the Qur'anic verse which says, "**Although eyes catch Him, He catches all eyes and He is Subtle and Aware.**"
    (e) the Prophet's saying that "*Each of you will see Allaah on the Day of Judgement and there will not be between you and Him a veil.*"

4. USOOL AT-TAFSEER: MAKKAN AND MADEENAN REVELATIONS

The Qur'aan was revealed in sections to Prophet Muhammad (ﷺ) from the beginning of his prophethood until shortly before his death. Thus, the Qur'aan came down continuously over a period of twenty-three years.

Many sections of the Qur'aan were generally revealed to solve the problems which existed among the Muslim communities in both Makkah and Madeenah. Since the problems and needs of Makkah were different from those of Madeenah, the revelations of Makkah and Madeenah have special characteristics of their own.

It is important to know the difference between the revelations of Makkah and Madeenah if the Qur'aan itself is to be clearly understood. Because of the great importance of the Qur'aan to Islaam, Muslim scholars from the time of the *Sahaabah* have devoted much time and effort in this area of study.

THE FEATURES OF MAKKAN REVELATIONS

Makkan revelations are defined as all verses and chapters of the Qur'aan which were brought by Jibreel to the Prophet (ﷺ) before the *Hijrah*[44] (622 C.E.). This includes verses which were revealed in Taa'if as well as those revealed in other areas outside of Makkah. These revelations represent the first stage of the Islamic movement in which its fundamentals were established.

1. Tawheed:

When Islaam was first presented to the people of Makkah, they were in a state of disbelief. Most of them believed in Allaah, but they had put between themselves and Allaah many intermediaries. They made idols to represent these intermediaries and worshipped them instead of Allaah. Thus, the early revelations taught the people about Allaah's unity and

---

[44] The emigration of the Prophet (ﷺ) to Madinah.

power over all things. They told the people that Allaah was without parents, offspring or any partner who shared His powers. They also pointed out that idols could neither bring good nor hold back evil. And they questioned the logic of worshipping things which could not even see or hear.

2. Salaah:

After the first verses of revelation came informing the Prophet (ﷺ) that he had been chosen for prophethood, Allaah sent Jibreel to teach him the correct method of prayer. This was necessary because the correct method of prayer could not be arrived at by logical reasoning. Therefore, even the Prophet (ﷺ) himself had to be taught the correct method of worshipping Allaah. Thus, the early verses called upon the Prophet (ﷺ) and his early band of followers to make their *Salaah* regularly.

Since the Makkans were in the habit of worshipping idols in the belief that these home-made gods would carry their prayers to Allaah for them, the early verses were also aimed at clarifying this misconception. The verses taught that *Salaah* should only be made for and to Allaah, as He is the only one who can answer them.

Great stress was placed on *Salaah* because of its relationship to *Tawheed*. Correct *Salaah* directed to Allaah alone is the most basic way of putting *Tawheed* into practice.

3. The Unseen:

Since there was no way that human beings could possibly come to know about the unseen world, the early verses taught them about its wonders, its mysteries, and its horrors. The verses described Paradise and its pleasures in order to encourage the believers to continue to do good deeds and to assure them of a reward. They also described the Hell-fire and its torments in order to encourage the believers to strive to avoid evil deeds. Descriptions of the fire and its inhabitants also reassured the believers that those who do wrong in this life will not escape Allaah's punishment. Such descriptions were also aimed at scaring the disbelievers into reconsidering their position before it became too late. Some of the verses also reasoned with those who could not accept the resurrection by giving them examples from nature, such as rain falling on dead earth bringing it back to life.

وَٱللَّهُ ٱلَّذِىٓ أَرۡسَلَ ٱلرِّيَٰحَ فَتُثِيرُ سَحَابًا فَسُقۡنَٰهُ إِلَىٰ بَلَدٍ مَّيِّتٍ فَأَحۡيَيۡنَا بِهِ ٱلۡأَرۡضَ بَعۡدَ مَوۡتِهَا كَذَٰلِكَ ٱلنُّشُورُ ۝

"And it is Allaah who sends the winds sturring the clouds and We drive them to the earth after its death. Likewise (will be) the Resurrection."

Soorah Faatir (35) : 9

Others pointed out logically that the recreation of life would be easier than its creation, although it is all the same to Allaah.

وَهُوَ ٱلَّذِى يَبۡدَؤُاْ ٱلۡخَلۡقَ ثُمَّ يُعِيدُهُۥ وَهُوَ أَهۡوَنُ عَلَيۡهِۚ

"And it is He who originates the creation, then recreates it (after it has perished) which is easier for Him...."

Soorah ar-Room (30) : 27

4. Allaah's Existence:

There were some individuals among the Makkans who were in doubt about Allaah's very existence. Thus, some of the early verses presented logical arguments proving Allaah's existence. Sometimes proofs were taken from nature and the creatures common to the society. Allaah asked the Makkans,

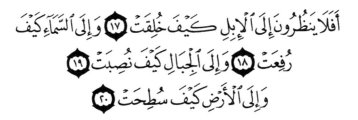

"Why didn't they look at the camels and how they were created, and the sky and how it was raised, and the mountains and how they are firmly fixed and the earth and how it was spread out?"

Soorah al-Ghaashiyah (88) : 17-20

At other times straight logic was used. Allaah asked them if they were created from nothing or if they created themselves:

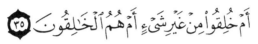

"Were they created of nothing, or were they themselves the creators?"

Soorah at-Toor (52) : 35

The answer had to be one or the other. Since they knew they had not created themselves, they had to realize that they were created. Even if they said that they came from their parents and their parents came from their parents and so on. The numbers eventually decrease to one who came from nothing. Thus, Allaah, the Creator, has to be accepted for our existence to make sense.

5. Challenges:

In order to prove to the Quraysh that the Qur'aan was from Allaah and that Muhammad (ﷺ) was a prophet of Allaah, some of the Makkan verses challenged the Arabs to imitate the Qur'aan. Many of the chapters began with individual letters like *"Alif, Laam* and *Meem," "Saad,"* or *"Noon"* in order to tease the Makkans with the same letters of the alphabet that they made their flowery speeches and poetry with. Allaah made the Qur'aan with the same letters, but they just could not imitate it. Since the Arabs were unable to produce even a chapter resembling the smallest chapter of the Qur'aan, the miraculous nature of the Qur'aan and its divine origin were clearly proven to the people at that time. However, many of them preferred to look at the Qur'aan as a magical spell, and the Prophet (ﷺ) as a master magician.

6. The People of Old:

The Makkan verses often mentioned historical examples of earlier civilizations, like the 'Aad and the *Thamood*. They were mentioned in order to warn those who had rejected the message of Islaam. The verses spoke about the wonders of the ancient civilizations. They listed the many blessings which Allaah had bestowed on the peoples of those civilizations. Then they recounted how the people disobeyed Allaah and denied His blessings, and how Allaah's punishment caught them when they were totally unaware of what could become of them if Allaah so willed. These examples were quite familiar to the Arabs because the ruins of such civilizations could still be seen. For example, the stone tombs of *Madaa' in Saalih* were directly on the trade route to Syria.

7. Eemaan:

Very few laws were revealed in the Makkan verses. Instead, the verses concentrated on principles which would build the *Eemaan* (faith) of the early Muslims. These verses spoke of the importance of fearing Allaah and being aware of His presence and knowledge of all things. They were often filled with advice about being patient, perseverant, truthful and trustworthy, in order to build the moral spiritual character of the early Muslims who were in a minority and under a lot of pressure from Makkan society.

8. Short Verses:

The Makkan *Soorahs* usually had short verses, catchy rhymes, and a very strong rhythm. These qualities were meant to catch the attention of listeners who were basically opposed to the message of Islaam. The verses had to be short because the audience would not be willing to listen to long, drawn-out statements. As soon as they heard any of the Qur'aan, they would stick their fingers in their ears and turn away. Thus, the verses often had to strike home immediately. They often resembled the chants of the oracles and fortunetellers, but their meanings were very clear, whereas the chants were mostly obscure and vague. For example, the oracle Zabraa warned her people about a disaster which would soon strike them as follows:

By the fluttering wind, and the falling night.
By the shining morn, and the piercing star.
By the rain-laden clouds,
Verily, the trees of the valley are really deceptive,
and teeth gnash until twisted.
Verily, the boulders of the mountain warn of mourning,
that you won't find any escape from.
The Fortuneteller Zabraa

THE FEATURES OF MADEENAN REVELATIONS

Madeenan revelations are all those verses and chapters of the Qur'aan which were revealed after the Hijrah. This includes verses which were revealed during the battles, as well as those revealed in Makkah and Minaa during and after the Farewell Pilgrimage. All of these verses are considered Madeenan because they represent the revelations of the second stage of the Islamic movement in which the consolidation of the Islamic state took place.

The following are some of the main characteristics of Madeenan verses:

1. Laws:

Once Madeenah had become the new center of the Islamic movement, the Islamic state was born. The Prophet (ﷺ) became ruler over the Muslims of Madeenah, as well as the Jews and the Arab idol worshippers who lived there. A constitution was drawn up and a system of justice was established. Thus, the verses during the Madeenan stage contained the many social, economic and spiritual laws which were necessary for the organization and development of an Islamic state. It was during this period that the last three pillars of Islaam, *Zakaah, Sawm* and *Hajj*, were revealed. Likewise, it was during this period that drinking alcohol, eating swine and gambling were all forbidden.

2. People of the Book:

In Madeenah, Muslims came in contact with the Jews for the first time. In order to try to shake the beliefs of the Muslims, the Jews used to ask the Prophet (ﷺ) various questions about Allaah, the earlier prophets, and the unseen. They asked questions about the origin of the soul and what it was made of. Thus, a number of Madeenan verses represented answers to the many questions raised by the Jews. The Muslims of Madeenah also came in contact with the Christians on a larger scale. As a result of that, we find a number of Madeenan verses clarifying Christian misconceptions about Prophet Jesus and Allaah. They pointed out that Jesus' birth was not greater than that of Aadam who had neither father nor mother.

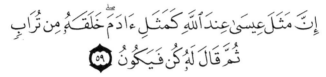

"Surely the likeness of Jesus in Allaah's sight is as the likeness of Aadam. He created him from dust, then said to him, 'Be!' And he was."

Soorah Aal-'Imraan (3) : 59

They also stressed that the miracles of Jesus, such as bringing the dead back to life, were only by Allaah's permission. Thus, Jesus was not a god nor the son of Allaah, and Allaah was not the third of three.

3. The Munaafiqoon:

For the first time since the beginning of the final message we find people entering Islaam, yet not believing in it. In Makkah, Muslims were oppressed and attacked, so no one would enter Islaam unless he truly believed. On the other hand, the Muslims of Madeenah were strong and they ruled the city. Thus, we find some people entering Islaam in order to benefit from its strength and to oppose it from within. 'Abdullaah ibn Ubayy ibn Salool was about to be crowned King of Madeenah when the Prophet (ﷺ) arrived. The Prophet (ﷺ) was made the ruler of Madeenah and Ibn Salool's hopes were ruined. Since the Muslims were strong and he could not openly oppose them, he accepted

Islaam and worked against it from within. He eventually became the head of the *Munaafiqoon* (hypocrites). Thus, the verses of the Madeenan stage warned the Muslims about the dangers of the hypocrites and taught them how to deal effectively with them.

4. Jihaad:

The right to fight against the enemy was given for the first time in al-Madeenah. During the Makkan period, Muslims were forbidden to fight back. This was for two basic reasons: (1) The Muslims were a minority and could easily be completely wiped out, and (2) only the strong could survive this test. The Makkan period prepared the foundation of the Islamic movement to come. It was during the Madeenan stage that a series of battles were fought against the forces of disbelief until finally Makkah was conquered and the whole of the Arabian peninsula came under the rule of Islaam. Thus, a number of the Madeenan verses taught Muslims the Islamic principles of war. For example, they taught how to deal with prisoners of war and they forbade retreat during an attack except as a trick to trap the enemy. They also encouraged the Muslims to prepare themselves with the best weapons and battle gear they could find.

5. Long Verses:

The Madeenan verses tended to be longer than those of Makkah. In fact, there are a number of Madeenan verses which are longer than whole soorahs of the Makkan period. The longest verse of the Qur'aan is the verse on loans[45] in the Madeenan *Soorah, al-Baqarah*. This verse contains approximately 143 words. The shortest *Soorah* of the Qur'aan is the Makkan *Soorah al-Kawthar*,[46] which contains a total of only 11 separate words in its three short verses. The need to catch the attention of unwilling listeners was no longer there because Islaam had become strong and its followers were many. Thus, the audience at this stage was quite willing to listen attentively to longer verses teaching the vital laws of Islam.

---

[45] Soorah al-Baqarah (2) : 292.
[46] The *Soorah* 102.

6. Order of the Soorahs:

Although all of the Makkan verses were revealed during the same period, they were neither memorized nor written in the same order in which they were revealed. Verses from various *Soorahs* were revealed at once. Whenever single verses were revealed at once. Whenever single verses were revealed, the Prophet (ﷺ) would tell his scribes to write it in the *Soorah* to which it belonged. If a new *Soorah* was revealed, he would recite the *Soorah* in the order it was to be recorded. Once the Madeenan verses and *Soorahs* began to be revealed, the Prophet (ﷺ) would tell his companions to place them before or after certain Makkan *Soorahs* and verses. Thus, when the revelation of the Qur'aan was complete, Makkan verses could be found within Madeenan *Soorahs* and Madeenan verses within Makkan *Soorahs*. The Prophet (ﷺ) reordered the verses and *Soorahs* of the Qur'aan according to Allaah's command. the reason for that was that the verses were revealed according to the needs of a developing community, whereas the order for reading purposes needed to be varied so as not to make the Qur'aan seem one-sided in its presentation. The mixture of verses and chapters from the two stages gives the reader a more balanced picture of the message of Islaam.

THE IMPORTANCE

There are a number of reasons why a distinction needs to be made between Makkan and Madeenan *Soorahs* and verses. The following are only the three most important reasons:

1. Fiqh (Islamic Law)

The various laws of Islaam were revealed over a period of twenty-three years. Some laws canceled earlier laws and other laws were revealed bit by bit. Thus, it is necessary to know at which point in time the various laws were revealed in order to apply them properly. The laws of the later Madeenan period sometimes took the place of earlier laws. For example, alcohol was made forbidden in gradual stages. The first law concerning alcohol was simply a warning of its dangers. Allaah said,

يَسْـَٔلُونَكَ عَنِ ٱلْخَمْرِ وَٱلْمَيْسِرِ قُلْ فِيهِمَا إِثْمٌ
كَبِيرٌ وَمَنَٰفِعُ لِلنَّاسِ وَإِثْمُهُمَا أَكْبَرُ مِن نَّفْعِهِمَا

"And, when they ask you about *Khamr* (alcohol) and *Maysir* (gambling), tell them that they contain benefit for some people, but the sin is greater than the benefit."

Soorah al-Baqarah (2) : 219

The second law which was revealed warned Muslims away from *Salaah* when they were intoxicated (drunk). Allaah said,

لَا تَقْرَبُوا۟ ٱلصَّلَوٰةَ وَأَنتُمْ سُكَٰرَىٰ حَتَّىٰ تَعْلَمُوا۟ مَا تَقُولُونَ

"Do not come to Salaah when you are intoxicated (drunk), until you know what you are saying."

Soorah an-Nisaa' (4) : 43

The third law, however, was a complete prohibition of even coming near any form of alcohol. Allaah said,

إِنَّمَا ٱلْخَمْرُ وَٱلْمَيْسِرُ وَٱلْأَنصَابُ وَٱلْأَزْلَٰمُ رِجْسٌ
مِّنْ عَمَلِ ٱلشَّيْطَٰنِ فَٱجْتَنِبُوهُ لَعَلَّكُمْ تُفْلِحُونَ

"Verily, alcohol, gambling and sacrificial altars are filth, as a result of Shaytaan's work, so stay away from them."

Soorah al-Maa'idah (5) : 93

If one was unaware of the order in which these verses were revealed, he or she may mistakenly think that drinking alcohol is allowed as long as one doesn't get drunk and come to Salaah. Or, it might be thought that benefitting from the sale of alcohol is permitted.

2. Da'wah

By understanding the order in which the verses of the Qur'aan were revealed, one can learn the best method of teaching Islaam. For example, the Qur'aan taught the believers not to curse or make fun of the idols of the disbelievers in order not to drive them away and in order that they do not curse Allaah out of ignorance. Instead they were told to reason with the disbelievers and show them logically why the worship of idols was incorrect. Allaah said,

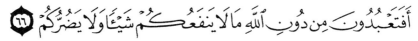

"Are you worshipping besides Allaah other gods which cannot benefit you at all nor harm you?"

Soorah al-Anbiyaa' (21) : 66

3. Seerah

Many of the important events in the Prophet's life have been recorded in various partsof the Qur'aan. Thus, by knowing the order in which the verses were revealed, it is possible to piece together a large portion of the biography of the Prophet (ﷺ).

QUESTIONS

1. Makkan revelations are
    (a) whatever the Prophet (ﷺ) said or did before the *Hijrah*.
    (b) the verses of the Qur'aan revealed in Makkah before the *Hijrah*.
    (c) sayings of the Prophet (ﷺ) in Makkah after the *Hijrah*.
    (d) Qur'anic verses revealed before the *Hijrah*.
    (e) verses of the Qur'aan revealed after the *Hijrah*, whether in Makkah or elsewhere.

2. Makkan and Madeenan revelations could be compared with regard to their length in one of the following ways:
    (a) Makkan verses were long because people wanted to hear about Islaam since it was new, while Madeenan verses were short because the people were already Muslims and only needed short explanations.
    (b) Verses revealed in Madeenah were long and Makkan verses were short because the people of Madeenah were mostly non Muslims and needed long explanations, while those who listened to the Qur'aan in Makkah were mostly Muslims, so short explanations were sufficient.
    (c) The verses revealed during the Makkan period were short in order to catch the attention of non-Muslim listeners who did not want to hear the Qur'aan, while the verses of Madeenah were long because the audience was mostly Muslims who were prepared to listen to long explanations.
    (d) Madeenan verses were short as a result of the need for a short, catchy style suited to the pagans of Madeenah who had no desire to listen to the Prophet (ﷺ) while Makkan verses were long because they were mostly directed to Muslims who were patient and willing to listen.
    (e) Makkan verses were long to explain the new religion to the pagan Quraysh, while Madeenan verses were short because the people of Madeenah were already Muslim and didn't need long explanations.

3. Makkan and Madeenan verses could be compared with respect to their general content in one of the following ways:

   (a) Makkan verses were mostly concerned with *Tawheed* (oneness of God) because Makkans were mostly pagans, while Madeenan verses were mostly concerned with Allaah's existence because many Madeenans were Christians.

   (b) Madeenan verses contained laws necessary for a developing Islamic state, while Makkan verses dealt with the questions and misconceptions of Jews and Christians.

   (c) Madeenan verses mostly concentrated on principles which would build the *Eemaan* (faith) of the early Muslims, while Makkan verses were mostly concerned with the social and economic laws required by a developing Islamic state.

   (d) Makkan verses spoke mainly about *Tawheed*, owing to widespread idol-worship among Makkans, while those of Madeenah taught the laws needed in the newly-formed Muslim state headed by the Prophet (ﷺ).

   (e) Madeenan verses mostly contained the laws needed for a developing Muslim state, while those of Makkah dealt with the *Munaafiqoon* (hypocrites) who had joined Islaam to destroy it from within.

4. Makkan and Madeenan revelations could be compared with regard to Jihaad in one of the following ways:

   (a) Makkan verses did not allow fighting and Madeenan verses ordered it, owing to the weak *Eemaan* of the early Muslims in Makkah and the need to build the foundation of faith among the Muslims of Madeenah.

   (b) Permission to fight did not come in the Makkan verses because the Muslims were few during that period and could easily be wiped out by their numerous enemies, while Madeenan verses allowed fighting since many Madeenans had accepted Islaam and Muslims were then able to resist the pagans.

   (c) Madeenan verses permitted fighting because Makkans were constantly attacking the Muslims of Madeenah, while Makkan verses did not since the Quraysh were not afraid of Muslims due to their small numbers, so there was no need to fight them.

(d) Verses revealed in Madeenah did not allow fighting because the Muslim state was being formed and most people in Madeenah were Muslims, while the verses of the Makkan period allowed fighting in order for Muslims to defend themselves against their pagan enemies.

(e) Makkan verses allowed fighting because the Muslims were always being persecuted and attacked by their enemies, while the verses of the Madeenan period forbade it because the Muslims were no longer being attacked.

5.The order of the chapters and verses of the Qur'aan was changed because

(a) the needs of the Makkan period were different from those of the Madeenan period, so the Makkan chapters were put at the end to make memorizing the Qur'aan easier.

(b) Makkan revelations were short and choppy, while Madeenan revelations were long and the long verses at the beginning.

(c) the Qur'aan was revealed to suit the needs of a developing community in Makkah, while in Madeenah another order was needed to avoid one-sidedness.

(d) the Qur'aan was not put together in one book during the Prophet's lifetime, and the _Sahaabah_ put it in the order they thought was best.

(e) the order for reading purposes needed a mixture of Makkan and Madeenan verses and chapters in order to avoid one-sidedness.

5. TAFSEER SOORAH AZ-ZILZAAL (99)

Name of the Soorah

The name "*Zilzaal*" (quake) is the gerund (verbal noun) from the verb "*Zalzala*" which occurs in the passive feminine form (*Zulzilat*) in the middle of the first verse of the Soorah. The name "*Zilzaal*" was not common to the Prophet (ﷺ) and his companions, as it was their practice to refer to the Soorahs by quoting either the complete first verse or the first few words from it. The practice of assigning names to the Soorahs was done at a much later time.

Place of Revelation

This *Soorah* was revealed after *Soorah* an-Nisaa' (4). Ibn 'Abbaas said that *Ethaa-zulzilat* was revealed in Madeenah,[47] but Ibn Mas'ood was of the opinion that it was revealed in Makkah. Because Ibn 'Abbaas was considered the greatest *Mufassir*[48] of the Qur'aan among the *Sahaabah*, his opinion concerning the place of revelation of this *Soorah* is considered to be more accurate than that of Ibn Mas'ood; thus, this *Soorah* is considered to be Madeenan.

Reason for Revelation

Allaah describes some of the signs of the Last Day in this *Soorah* in order to warn man of the coming end of the world. Allaah further explains that all deeds will be judged and all secrets exposed. Consequently, man is advised to do as much good as he can to fill his scale of righteous deeds at the time of judgement.

Hadeeth Concerning this Soorah

Anas reported that the Prophet (ﷺ) said, "*Whoever recites 'Ethaa-zulzilaatil-ard' is given a reward equal to reciting half of the Qur'aan.*

---

[47] *Fat-h al-Qadeer*, vol.5, p.478.

[48] A person who makes a *Tafseer*, or explanation of the meaning of the Qur'aan.

SOORAH AZ-ZILZAAL

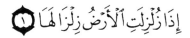

1. When the earth is shook mightily

Almighty Allaah proceeds in this Soorah to paint for us a picture of the Last Hour in order that we might reflect on the passing nature of this world and concentrate on what really counts in it. He starts the picture with the mighty heaving and shuddering of the earth's crust as it slows down and approaches a final end. The globe is rocked with devastating earthquakes in all of its corners, causing everything to crack and splinter into pieces, leaving nothing as it was.

The sinking of large sections of the earth is among the major signs of the approach of the Last Hour which were prophesied by the final messenger of God. Huthayfah ibn Usayd reported that on one occasion the Prophet (ﷺ) came to them while they were busy in discussion and asked, *"About what are you discussing?" They replied, "We were discussing about the Last Hour." He then said, "It will not come until you see ten signs: the smoke (Qur'aan 44:10); Dajjaal (the false Christ); the beast (Qur'aan 27 :82); the rising of the sun in the West; the descent of Jesus; the Gog and the Magog; and the sinking of land in three locations, in the East, the West and in Arabia, followed by a huge fire which would begin in Yemen and drive people to their place of assembly."*[49]

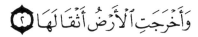

2. And the earth expels its burdens

Allaah, Most Great, continues to describe the awesome events which will befall the earth, one after another, while the surface of the earth crumbles and cracks. Corpses and remains of the dead will spew and pour out of their graves and onto its surface. Wherever anyone died, he will be recovered, whether it is from the depths of the ocean, amidst

---

[49]   Collected by Muslim (*Sahih Muslim* (English Trans.), vol.4, pp. 1503-1504, no.6931, Abu Daawood and at-Tirmithee.

the towering mountains, or even if the body was reduced to ashes and scattered, as done by the Hindus.

In other chapters of the Qur'aan, Allaah describes some of the other events which will be happening in the heavens and the seas:

"When the sky cracks; and the planets scatter; and the seas explode; and the graves are overturned"
Soorah Infitaar (82) : 1-4

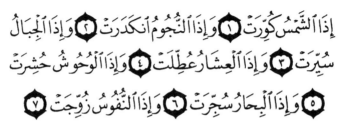

"When the sun is folded and loses its light; and the stars fall; and the mountains disintegrate;... and the seas are ignited; and the souls are rejoined with their bodies."
Soorah at-Takweer (81) : 1-3, 6-7.

The stage is now being set for the final judgement, and all that was hidden in this world will be exposed. This refers also to our hidden deeds and intentions, which Allaah may have covered in this life, but will expose and judge on the Last Day. However, not everyone's faults will be exposed on that day. Allaah's mercy will cover the true believers. Abu Hurayrah mentioned that the Prophet (ﷺ) said, *"The righteous servant whose faults Allaah conceals in this world, will also have his faults concealed by Allaah on the Day of Resurrection."*[50]

---

[50] Collected by Muslim (*Sahih Muslim* (English Trans.), vol.4, p.1369, no.6266).

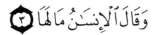

3. All men will say, "What is happening to it?"

Those remaining humans caught in the continual earthquakes and eruptions will cry out in horror as they see before their very eyes graves upturned and their contents poured out around them. They madly ask themselves and those around them, "What in the world is going on?" Those who will be caught alive on the Last Day are the most corrupt and degenerate of mankind according to the Prophet's statement, *"The Last Hour will not come except upon the most evil of mankind."*[51] The Prophet (ﷺ) was quoted by his wife 'Aa'ishah as saying, *"Allaah will send a fragrant wind by which everyone who has even a mustard seed's weight of faith will die, and only those who have no goodness will survive. They will then revert to the pagan religions of their forefathers."*[52] The people will go back to worshipping idols as their ancestors did and will forget all about the final hour and its signs. Abu Hurayrah reported that the Prophet (ﷺ) said, *"The Last Hour will not come until the women of the Daws tribe will be seen going around the idol of Thul-Khalasah in (pagan worship).*[53]

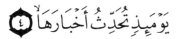

4. On that day it will reveal its secrets.

The earth will inform them of the secret behind all of this disruption and destruction. This secret was at one time common knowledge to most people, but later it became lost as disbelief spread, until the whole earth became enveloped in darkness. 'Abdullaah and Abu Moosaa quoted the Prophet (ﷺ) as saying, *"Before the Last Hour, there will be a time when knowledge will be taken away and ignorance will take its place; and bloodshed will take place on a very large scale."* The earth will tell them in its own way that the final judgement has arrived and the time for answering for all that was done in this life has come. Allaah said,

---

[51] Collected by Muslim (*Sahih Muslim* (English Trans.), vol.6, p.1526, no.7043).
[52] Collected by Muslim (*Sahih Muslim* (English Trans.), vol.4, p.1506, no.6945).
[53] Collected by Muslim (*Sahih Muslim* (English Trans.), vol.4, p.1506, no.6944).

وَإِذَا وَقَعَ ٱلْقَوْلُ عَلَيْهِمْ أَخْرَجْنَا لَهُمْ دَآبَّةً مِّنَ ٱلْأَرْضِ
تُكَلِّمُهُمْ أَنَّ ٱلنَّاسَ كَانُوا۟ بِـَٔايَـٰتِنَا لَا يُوقِنُونَ ﴿٨٢﴾

"And when the word is fulfilled against them, we will bring out of the earth a beast which will speak to them, because mankind did not believe in Our signs."

Soorah an-Naml (27) : 82

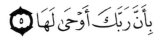

5. Because your Lord has permitted it.

It is by Allaah's permission that the earth will inform the last of mankind of the cause of all that devastation and the expulsion of the dead shortly before the earth itself is destroyed. It might seem strange to us that the earth will speak. But Allaah is able to make all of His creation speak as He has informed us:

حَتَّىٰٓ إِذَا مَا جَآءُوهَا شَهِدَ
عَلَيْهِمْ سَمْعُهُمْ وَأَبْصَـٰرُهُمْ وَجُلُودُهُم بِمَا كَانُوا۟ يَعْمَلُونَ ﴿٢٠﴾
وَقَالُوا۟ لِجُلُودِهِمْ لِمَ شَهِدتُّمْ عَلَيْنَا قَالُوٓا۟ أَنطَقَنَا ٱللَّهُ ٱلَّذِىٓ
أَنطَقَ كُلَّ شَىْءٍ

"....When they reach (the fire) their ears, eyes and skins will testify against them about what they did. And they will ask their skins, "Why do you testify against us?' They will say, 'Allaah, who causes all things to speak, has caused us to speak...'"

Soorah Fussilat (41) : 20-21

يَوْمَئِذٍ يَصْدُرُ ٱلنَّاسُ أَشْتَاتًا لِّيُرَوْا۟ أَعْمَـٰلَهُمْ ﴿٦﴾

6. On that day man will return as individuals and will be shown their deeds.

When all the preceding events take place, all mankind will return from the state of death as individuals, no one recognizing the other. All earthly ties will be broken and each will only be concerned with himself. Allaah describes this as:

"A day when man will flee from his brother, his mother, his father, his wife, and his children. Each of them that day will have enough concern of his own to make him indifferent to the others."

Soorah 'Abasa (80) : 34-37

Allaah will cause them all to come face to face with all that they did in their lives in order that the basis of His judgement will be undisputed and the supremacy of His justice will prevail. Almighty Allaah said:

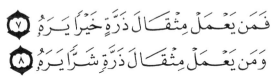

"...'Read your book. You are sufficient to call yourself to account.'"

Soorah al-Israa' (17) : 14-15

7. Whoever does an ant's weight of good will see it,
8. And whoever does an ant's weight of evil will see it.

Allaah uses the word _Tharrah_ (the smallest ant) to indicated that no matter how insignificant and small an act of good or evil may be, it has all been recorded by the angels of the right and left, and on that day the complete records will be presented before us. Therefore, we should not consider any good deed as being of no value, but instead we should strive to accomplish all the good we can as it will not be lost or forgotten. The Prophet (ﷺ) urged us to do all we could saying, _"Don't scorn_ *any form of good, do it even if it is only meeting your brother with a smiling face."*[54]

Every opportunity to point out a good deed should be utilized because the Prophet (ﷺ) also informed us that, *"whoever points out a good deed gets the same reward as the one who does it."*[55]

---

[54] Collected by Muslim (*Sahih Muslim* (English Trans.), vol.4, p.1383, no.6359.

[55] Reported by Abu Hurayrah and collected by Muslim (*Sahih Muslim* (English Trans.) vol.4, pp.1405-6, nos. 6466 and 6470) and Abu Daawood (*Sunan Aboo Daawood* (English Trans.), vol.3, p.1420, no.5110).

QUESTIONS

1. The literal meaning of the word *zilzaal* is
   (a) the knocker.
   (b) a bottomless pit.
   (c) an earthquake.
   (d) the Day of Judgement.
   (e) the Hellfire.

2. In *Soorah al-zilzaal*, the title *zilzaal* refers to
   (a) the breaking up of the earth on the Day of Judgement.
   (b) the Day of Judgement itself.
   (c) the Hellfire.
   (d) a thing which knocks.
   (e) Allaah's judgement.

3. In the verse " On that day it will reveal its secrets," the word "secrets" refers to
   (a) the dead bodies coming our of their graves.
   (b) the earthquakes which tear up the earth.
   (c) the arrival of the Day of Judgement.
   (d) the wind which will take the souls of the believers.
   (e) none of the above.

4. The reason why Allaah will show everyone their deeds is to
   (a) find out who were the true believers and who were not.
   (b) terrify mankind and make them all believe in Him.
   (c) show man that the Day of Judgement is real.
   (d) convince man that he deserves whatever he receives on the Day do Judgement.
   (e) weigh them on the scales of justice.

5. *In Soorah al-zilzaal*, Allaah refers to an ant's weight of good and evil in order to

(a) show that even ants will be judged on the Last Day.

(b) indicate that extremely small acts of good and evil do not count.

(c) inform man that small acts of good will be recorded in his favor, while small acts of evil will not be held against him.

(d) show that any deed weighing less than an ant will not be counted for or against man.

(e) indicate that even the smallest acts of good and evil will be recorded for and against man

6. The significance of men being resurrected as individuals as mentioned in *Soorah al-zilzaal* is

(a) to remind man that he will be judged by himself with no one to help him.

(b) to scare man into finding out where he is going to die.

(c) to encourage the believers to have themselves buried near other believers.

(d) to inform man that everyone will get a chance to see Allaah by himself on the Day of Judgement.

(e) none of the above.

6. TAFSEER SOORAH AL-QAARI‘AH (101)

Name of the Soorah

Qaari‘ah literally means a thing which knocks or strikes. The Arabs used to say, "the *Qaari‘ah* struck" if a disaster occurred.

There is some difference of opinion as to whether this *Soorah* has 10 or 11 verses. Some scholars consider verses 1 and 2 to be a single verse, while others consider them separate verses. Actually, the verses of the Qur’aan were not numbered in the early Qur’anic manuscripts because the Prophet (ﷺ) did not specify them. The only chapter of the Qur’aan which the Prophet (ﷺ) specified the number of verses for is *Soorah al-Faatihah*.

Place of Revelation

This *Soorah* was revealed after *Soorah Quraysh* (106). Ibn Mardawayh collected a narration that Ibn ‘Abbaas said, "*Soorah al-Qaari‘ah* was revealed in Makkah."

Reason for Revelation

Soorah al-Qaari‘ah describes for the Makkan pagans, and for mankind in general, some of the scenes of the Day of Resurrection. It explains some of the horrors of that day and the helplessness of mankind in order to make man reflect on his end. The final day will come when man least expects it, like a knocker at his door. Thus, he is encouraged to prepare for that day by accepting true faith and by doing righteous deeds.

SOORAH AL-QAARI‘AH

1. Al-Qaari‘ah 2. What is al-Qaari‘ah?

In this Soorah, Allaah takes the idiom *al-Qaari'ah* (the knocker) and uses it to create wonder, amazement, worry and fear in the mind of the listener. This was especially important in Makkah in the early days of Islaam because the pagan Makkans would not listen to the Qur'aan. Allaah is asking them what is really the Qaari'ah, and also pointing out that it is not as they had been thinking, but in fact it is much more serious.

وَمَآ أَدْرَىٰكَ مَا ٱلْقَارِعَةُ ٣

3. And what will make you understand what the Qaari'ah is?

Allaah asks another rhetorical question about *al-Qaari'ah* to increase to increase in the listener's mind curiosity about this particular *Qaari'ah*. He does it as if to say that this *Qaari'ah* is far beyond man's ability to comprehend. It is in fact, so strange and horrible that man's mind cannot grasp its full meaning, so Allaah goes on to tell about some of its signs.

يَوْمَ يَكُونُ ٱلنَّاسُ كَٱلْفَرَاشِ ٱلْمَبْثُوثِ ٤

4. (It is) a day when men will be like scattered moths.

Al-Qaari'ah is a day when all mankind will be scattered over all parts of the earth, covering every square inch of it like a swarm of moths or bees.

All of the generations of man, from Adam's time until the Last Day will be brought back to life by Allaah's command. No matter how far and wide their remains have spread, whether re-absorbed by the earth, blown by the winds or swept away by rivers and seas, on Allaah's single command "*Kun*,"[56] all will be recombined and every soul will be reclothed in their bodies in preparation for the final judgement.

The Prophet's wife 'Aa'ishah quoted the Messenger of Allaah (ﷺ) as saying, "*Mankind will be gathered barefooted, naked and uncircum-*

---

[56] "Be!"

cised," She asked, *"O Messenger of Allaah, will the men and women stare at each other?" "O 'Aa'ishah,"* he replied, *"the circumstance will be much too fearful for any of them to look at each other."*[57]

People will be so afraid that they will almost drown in their sweat. Ibn 'Umar related concerning the verse, **"A Day when mankind will stand before the Lord of the worlds"**[58] that the Prophet (ﷺ) said, *"They will stand submerged in sweat up to the middle of their ears."*[59] Allaah's Messenger (ﷺ) was quoted by Miqdaad ibn Aswad as saying, *"On the Day of Resurrection, the sun will come so close to people that only the distance of one mile will be left. People will be submerged in perspiration according to their deeds, some up to their knees, some up to their waist, and some will have a bridle of perspiration up to—"* and while saying this, Allaah's Messenger (ﷺ) pointed to his mouth.[60]

5.   And the mountains will be like multi-coloured fluffed wool.

On that day the earth will become unrecognizable, its features changed as if by a child's paint brush, its familiarity totally lost. In *Soorah Ibraaheem,* verse 48, Allaah said, **"On the Day when the earth will be changed to another earth and likewise the heavens."** It will be a strange new world. The mountains which in this world appear to be unaffected by time and stand their guard solidly, in the new earth will be turned to dust and will be scattered like puffs of sheep's wool in many different colours. Allaah gave some the these details in other verses of the Qur'aan like:

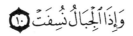

---

[57] Collected by al-Bukhaaree (*Sahih al-Bukhari* (Arabic-English), vol.8, p.350, no.534) and Muslim (*Sahih Muslim* (English Trans.), vol.4, p.1486, no.6844).

[58] Soorah al-Mutaffifeen (83) : 6.

[59] Collected by al-Bukhaaree (*Sahih al-Bukhari* (Arabic-English), vol.8, p.354, no.538) and Muslim (*Sahih Muslim* (English Trans.), vol.4, p.1487, no.6849).

[60] Collected by Muslim (*Sahih Muslim* (English Trans.), vol.4, pp.1487-1488, no.6852.

"And when the mountains are blown away."

Soorah al-Musalaat (77) : 10

"And the mountains will be moved from their places and become a mirage."

Soorah an-Naba' (78) : 20

"And the mountains will be crumbled to pieces and become floating dust particles."

Soorah Waaqi'ah (56) : 5-6

The new earth will become completely flat and completely devoid of any landmarks. Sahl ibn Sa'd related that he heard the Prophet (ﷺ) say, *"On the Day of Resurrection mankind will be gathered on a reddish-white plain looking like a loaf of flat bread."* Sahl added, *"The land will have no landmarks for anybody to recognize."*[61]

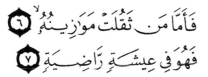

6 & 7. Whoever's scales are heavy then will have a pleasing life.

Allaah, in this verse, lays down the rules by which the judgement will be made. All of the actions which man does in this life will be put in the scales of justice in order to be weighed; good acts on one side of the scales and bad ones of the other. If the quality and quantity of good deeds are heavy enough to outweigh the evil ones, one is guaranteed and eternal life of bliss in which all that one desires will be his. But at the time of setting up of the scales, people will be so fearful that they will forget their loved ones and friends. *'Aaishah reported that she remembered the fire and wept. Allaah's Messenger (ﷺ) asked her, 'what*

---

[61] Collected by al-Bukhaaree (*Sahih al-Bukhari* (Arabic-English), vol.8, p.347, no.528.

is causing you to cry?" She replied, *"I thought about the fire and cried. Will you remember your family (i.e. your wives) on the Day of Resurrection?"* The Prophet (ﷺ) said, *"There are three places where no one will remember anyone else: at the scale, until he knows whether his scales will be light or heavy; at the Record, until it is said, 'Come and read your record' until he knows whether the record will fall in his right hand or in his left or from behind his back; and at at the Bridge when it is placed between the two sides of hell."*[62]

8 & 9 As for he whose scales are light, his mother will then be the abyss (Haawiyah).

If, on the other hand man's evil deeds outweigh his good deeds, Paradise will be placed beyond his grasp and he will be dragged screaming and crying to the edge of *Haawiyah,* a bottomless pit. He will then be hurled headlong into its outstretched arms. As he falls into it endlessly, it closes around him in a tight embrace, like a mother hugging her child.

10. What will inform you of what it is?

By repeating this haunting rhetorical question which brings to mind the worst of fears, Allaah tells us that this *Haawiyah* is so terrible that mere human words cannot convey its reality.

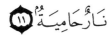

11. A fiercely blazing fire.

The closest thing in this world to describe the *Haawiyah,* the future mother of the wretched, is a super-heated fire which melts flesh and

---

[62] Collected by Abu Daawood (*Sunan Abu Dawud* (English Trans.), vol.3, p. 1331, no.4737) and authenticated by al-Arnaa'oot in *Jaami' al-Usool,* vol.10, pp.474-475, no.8008. See also *al-Hadis,* vol.4, p.119, no.27.

bones and sears the very soul. Abu Hurayrah reported that Allaah's Messenger (ﷺ) said, *"The fire of your world is one-seventieth of the Hellfire."* Someone said, *"O Messenger of Allaah, the fire of this world would have been sufficient to torture the disbelievers."* The Prophet (ﷺ) said, *"The Hellfire is sixty-nine times more hot."* [63] The Hellfire is so hot that even an ember from it will cause a man's body to burn. An-Nu'maan ibn Basheer quoted the Prophet (ﷺ) as saying, *"Among the people of Hell, the person with the least punishment on the Day of Judgement will be a man under the arch of whose feet an ember will be placed which will cause his brain to boil."* [64] So the Hellfire is not something to be taken lightly. It is something to be feared by doing righteous deeds and avoiding sin. Otherwise, all who enter it will regret as none have ever regretted before. The Prophet (ﷺ) was reported to have said, *"Allaah will say to the person with the least punishment in the fire on the Day of Judgement, 'If you possessed everything on earth, would you use them to ransom yourself (from the fire)?' He will reply, ' Yes.' And Allaah will say, 'I wanted much less then this from you while you were in the loins of Aadam: that you should not worship any gods besides Me, but you refused and worshipped other gods besides Me.'"* [65] This is why the Prophet (ﷺ) warned us saying, *"Protect yourselves from the fire, even it is (by giving in charity) half a date. And one who does not even have this should do so by saying a good and pleasant word."* [66]

Haawiyah is, in fact, one of the many names with which Allaah has referred to *Jahannam* (Hell), and al-Qaari'ah is among the names of *Qiyaamah* (Day of Resurrection). Haawiyah means abyss or bottomless pit which is a description of one of the scary features of the Hellfire. 'Utbah ibn Ghazwaan said," *...It was mentioned to us that a stone*

---

[63] Collected by al-Bukhaaree (*Sahih al-Bukhari* (Arabic English), vol.4, p.315, no.487) and Muslim (*Sahih Muslim* (English Trans.), vol.4, p.1482, no.6811).

[64] Collected by al-Bukhaaree.

[65] Collected by al-Bukhaaree (*Sahih al-Bukhari* (Arabic-English), vol.8, p.366, no. 562).

[66] Collected by al-Bukhaaree (*Sahih al-Bukhari* (Arabic-English), vol.8, pp.358-359, no.548).

will be thrown from the edge of Hell and it would fall for seventy years and not reach the bottom..."[67]

Allaah uses these various names to bring out some of the more terrifying features of the next life in order to shock man into reflecting on his end and thus try to set his present life in order.

The greatest deed that one can do is to sincerely believe and declare one's faith in the One True God, Allaah, and in the Messenger of Allaah (صلى الله عليه وسلم) who brought Islaam to mankind. This is the only act which will ensure man's salvation. It is the only thing which can save mankind from Hell. However, saying the words of faith like the way that a parrot repeats the words of its owner will not benefit us in the least. It is true faith in what is said which will be of use to us on the Day of Resurrection. 'Abdullaah ibn 'Amr reported that the Messenger of Allaah (صلى الله عليه وسلم) said, "*Allaah will take out a man from my nation in front of creation and spread before him ninety-nine scrolls, each scroll as long as the eye can see. Then He will say, 'Do you deny anything in it? Have My recording angels wronged You?' 'No my Lord' will be his reply. Allaah will then say, 'No. I have a good deed for you, and you will not be wronged on this day.' A sentence from the scroll containing* **Ashhadu al-laa ilaaha il-lal-laah wa ash-hadu anna Muhammadan 'Abduhoo wa rasooluh** *(I bear witness that there is no god worthy of worship but Allaah and I bear witness that Muhammad is His slave and messenger) will be removed. Allaah will say, 'Be present at the weighing of your deeds.' The man will say, 'O Lord, what is this sentence in comparison to these scrolls?' Allaah will say, 'You will not be wronged.' The scrolls will become light and the sentence heavy for nothing is heavier than Allaah's name.*"[68]

---

[67] Collected by Muslim (*Sahih Muslim* (English Trans.), vol.4, p. 1532, no.7075).

[68] Collected by Ibn Maajah and at-Tirmithee (*Al-Hadis*, vol.4, pp. 118-119, no.26) and authenticated in *Saheeh Sunan at-Tirmithee,* vol.2., pp.333-334, no.2127.

If man's evil deeds are many, he will be put in Hell, even though he declared his faith. However, he will be removed from Hell after he has been purified by the fire. The Prophet (ﷺ) was quoted by Abu Sa'eed al-Khudree as saying, "*When the people of Paradise have entered Paradise and the people of Hell have entered Hell, Allaah will then say, 'Take out of the fire whoever has a mustard seed's weight of faith in his heart.' They will come out, but by that time they will be burnt to coal. They will then be thrown into the river of life and they will spring up like the way a seed grows on the bank of a stream.*"[69] Such is the power of faith.

---

[69] Collected by al-Bukhaaree (*Sahih al-Bukhari* (Arabic English), vol.8, pp.367-368, no.565.

QUESTIONS

1. There is a difference of opinion about the number of verses in *Soorah al-Qaari'ah* because
    (a) the Prophet (ﷺ) specified the number of verses, but people forgot.
    (b) the Prophet (ﷺ) considered verses one and two as one verses.
    (c) the Prophet (ﷺ) did not specify the number of verses in it.
    (d) the Prophet (ﷺ) wanted the Soorah to match the Qur'aan in the heavens.
    (e) the Sahaabah did not specify the number of verses.

2. *Soorah al-Qaari'ah* is no longer in the order in which it was revealed
    (a) to inspire fear, worry and amazement in the minds of the listeners.
    (b) to increase its impact on the minds of the listeners.
    (c) because the Prophet (ﷺ) wanted the short Soorahs at the end of the Qur'aan.
    (d) because the Sahaabah ordered it to be changed to match the order in the heavens.
    (e) none of the above.

3. The literal meaning of the word *Qaari'ah* is
    (a) the Day of Judgement.
    (b) the Hellfire.
    (c) a bottomless pit.
    (d) a thing which jumps or hops.
    (e) a knocker.

4. The name *al-Qaari'ah* in this *Soorah* refers to
    (a) a disaster.
    (b) the Day of Judgement.
    (c) a thing which knocks.
    (d) the earthquakes at the end of the world.
    (e) the Hellfire.

5. "*Light scales*" in this *Soorah* refers to
    (a) a situation in which one's good deeds have outweighed one's bad deeds.
    (b) one's scales of good and bad deeds are nearly empty.
    (c) the scales of light used to measure good and bad deeds.
    (d) one's bad deeds have outweighed one's good deeds.
    (e) the scales of bad deeds are nearly empty.

6. *Haawiyah* literally means
    (a) a thing which knocks or strikes.
    (b) the Day of Judgement.
    (c) Hellfire.
    (d) a bottomless pit.
    (e) Paradise.

7. In *Soorah al-Qaari'ah* the word *Haawiyah* refers
    (a) the Hellfire.
    (b) man's evil deeds.
    (c) a pit.
    (d) Paradise.
    (e) the Day of Judgement.

8. Names like *Haawiyah* and *al-Qaari'ah* were used to
    (a) confuse the reader and the listener.
    (b) make the verses rhyme better.
    (c) bring out some of the more pleasurable aspects of the next life.
    (d) confuse the believers and scare the disbelievers.
    (e) explain some of the more terrifying features of the next life.

9. *Haawiyah* is described as a mother because
    (a) it will close around the believers like a mother hugs her child.
    (b) it embraces the disbelievers and feeds them like a mother does.
    (c) the believers run to it like a child runs to his mother.
    (d) those who fall in it are mostly children.
    (e) it closes around those who fall in it like a mother hugs her child

7. TAFSEER SOORAH AT-TAKAATHUR (102)

Name of the Soorah

At-Takkathur literally means " accumulation," and it was taken as a name from the first verse of the *Soorah*. This name was not, however, revealed, as is obvious from the Prophet's reference to the Soorah as '*Al-haakumut-takaathur,*" which is its first verse.

Place of Revelation

This *Soorah* was revealed immediately after *Soorah al-Kawthar* (108). Ibn Mardawayh collected a narration of Ibn 'Abbaas in which he said, "*Al-haakumut-takkaathur* was revealed in Makkah."[70]

Reason for Revelation

Allaah invites mankind to give up the worship of this world because such worship blinds them to the realities of this life. The early Muslims of Makkah were mostly poor and oppressed, so Allaah encouraged them to be steadfast in their faith and not to allow the riches, when they come, to divert them from their duties to God. They were reminded that this life is short and that they will have to answer for what they did with the blessing of Allaah.

'Amr ibn,'Awf related that the Ansaar[71] heard of Abu 'Ubaydah's arrival with *Zakaah* from Bahrain and after the *Fajr* prayer they came to the Prophet (ﷺ) who smiled and said, "*I think you have heard about the arrival of Abu 'Ubaydah and that he has brought something?*" They replied, "*Yes, O Messenger of Allaah.*" He said, "*The is good news, so hope for what will please you. By Allaah, I am not afraid that you will become poor, but I am afraid that the wordly wealth will be given to you in abundance as it was given to those nations before you, and you*

---

[70] *Fat-h al-Qadeer*, vol. 5, p.487.
[71] Companions of the Prophet (ﷺ) who were from Madeenah. They supported the Prophet (ﷺ) and his followers from Makkah when they emigrated to Madeenah. The Arabic word "*Ansaar*" means "helper" or "supporter."

will start competing with each other for it as they did, and then it will divert you as it did them." [72]

Hadeeths Concerning This Soorah

Ibn 'Umar reported that Allaah's Messenger (ﷺ) asked, *"Aren't any of you able to recite a thousand verses (of Qur'aan) daily?"* The companions replied, *"Who amongst us is able to recite 1,000 verses daily?"* He replied, *"Aren't any of you able to recite* **'Al-haakumut-takaathur'?"**[73]

'Abdullaah ibn ash-Shakh-kheer related that he came to the Messenger of Allaah (ﷺ) while he was reciting *"Al-haakumut-takaathur"* and he said, *Man says, 'My wealth, my wealth.'* But, O son of Aadam, do you have any of your wealth except what you have eaten and used, worn and worn out, and what you have given in charity and thereby cause it to remain?"[74]

SOORAH AT-TAKAATHUR

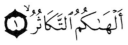

1. Accumulation diverts you.

In this *Soorah*, Allaah warns us to avoid certain habits of this life which have no real value besides temporary amusement. Man often spends his waking hours busily amassing wealth, children and fame in order to boast to others and rule the weak and helpless. This pointless activity blinds him to the realities of this life. He fails to realize that wealth, children, fame, etc. are only tests as Allaah stated,

$$وَٱعْلَمُوٓاْ أَنَّمَآ أَمْوَٰلُكُمْ وَأَوْلَٰدُكُمْ فِتْنَةٌ وَأَنَّ ٱللَّهَ عِندَهُۥٓ أَجْرٌ عَظِيمٌ ﴿٢٨﴾$$

---

[72] Collected by al-Bukhaaree (*Sahih al-Bukhari* (Arabic-English), vol.8, pp.289-290, no.433).

[73] Collected by al-Haakim and al-Bayhaqee in *Shu'ab al-Eemaan*.

[74] Collected by Muslim (*Sahih Muslim* (English Trans.), vol.4, p.1529, no.7061.

**"Know that verily your wealth and children are only
a trial and with Allaah is a great reward."**

Soorah al-Anfaal (8) : 28

By these tests and trials Allaah separates the believers from the non-believers and by them He also puts the believers on different levels according to their faith. Allaah said,

$$يَٰٓأَيُّهَا ٱلَّذِينَ ءَامَنُوا۟ لَا تُلْهِكُمْ$$

$$أَمْوَٰلُكُمْ وَلَآ أَوْلَٰدُكُمْ عَن ذِكْرِ ٱللَّهِ$$

**"O Believers, don't let your wealth or your children
divert you from the remembrance of Allaah."**

Soorah al-Munaafiqoon (63) : 9

The drive to amass more makes man forget the real purpose of his life, which is the worship of Allaah, and it also makes him forget that he will have to answer to Allaah for his deeds on the Day of Judgement. Thus, Allaah reminds us:

$$فَلَا تُعْجِبْكَ أَمْوَٰلُهُمْ وَلَآ أَوْلَٰدُهُمْ إِنَّمَا يُرِيدُ ٱللَّهُ لِيُعَذِّبَهُم$$

$$بِهَا فِي ٱلْحَيَوٰةِ ٱلدُّنْيَا وَتَزْهَقَ أَنفُسُهُمْ وَهُمْ كَٰفِرُونَ ۝$$

**"Do not let their wealth and children amaze you, for
Allaah only wants to punish them with it in this life
and that their souls be taken while they were disbelievers."**

Soorah at-Tawbah (9) : 55

Those who fail these tests have allowed their wives and children to become their own personal enemies without realizing it. Yet, Allaah tells us in the Qur'aan:

$$إِنَّ مِنْ أَزْوَٰجِكُمْ وَأَوْلَٰدِكُمْ عَدُوًّا لَّكُمْ فَٱحْذَرُوهُمْ$$

**"Surely there is in your wives and children an enemy
for you, so beware."**

Soorah at-Taghaabun (64) : 14

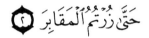 حَتَّىٰ زُرْتُمُ ٱلْمَقَابِرَ ٢

2. Until you visit the graveyards

The diversion created by the accumulation of this world's pleasures continues to trick many people into believing that everything is all right, until death catches up with them in this state of manifest ignorance.

فَلَمَّا نَسُوا مَا ذُكِّرُوا بِهِ فَتَحْنَا عَلَيْهِمْ أَبْوَابَ كُلِّ شَىْءٍ حَتَّىٰ إِذَا فَرِحُوا بِمَا أُوتُوا أَخَذْنَهُمْ

"So when they forgot (the warning) with which they were reminded, we opened to them the gates of every (pleasant) thing, until in the midst of their enjoyment in that which they were given, all of the sudden, we caught them..."

Soorah al-An'aam (6) : 44

It is only on their death beds that they finally awaken from their dream world of fun and games, but then it is too late. Even if they ask for forgiveness at that time it will not be accepted, as it was being sought in a state of fear at a time when the realities of the afterlife are evident. Allaah said,

وَلَيْسَتِ ٱلتَّوْبَةُ لِلَّذِينَ يَعْمَلُونَ ٱلسَّيِّئَاتِ حَتَّىٰ إِذَا حَضَرَ أَحَدَهُمُ ٱلْمَوْتُ قَالَ إِنِّي تُبْتُ ٱلْـَٰٔنَ

"There is no repentance for those who continue to do evil until death comes upon one of them and he says, 'Indeed, I have now repented,'...."

Soorah an-Nisaa' (4) : 18

'Abdullaah ibn 'Umar quoted the Prophet (ﷺ) as saying, *"Allaah, Most Great and Glorious, will accept His servant's repentance until his death rattle begins."*

They will beg for another chance, but Allaah said,

وَلَن يُؤَخِّرَ ٱللَّهُ نَفْسًا إِذَا جَآءَ أَجَلُهَا وَٱللَّهُ خَبِيرُۢ بِمَا تَعْمَلُونَ

"Allaah will not delay a soul if their appointed time comes, and Allaah knows all that you do."

Soorah Munaafiqoon (63) : 11

Greed is a very dangerous emotion because it is never satisfied. The more wealth and pleasure people have, the more they want. Only death finally and suddenly ends this desire. Both Ibn 'Abbaas and Anas reported that the Prophet (ﷺ) said, *"If one of Adam's descendants had a valley of gold, he would wish for two valleys, for nothing will end his greed except the dirt of his grave."*[75] The believers are therefore advised to avoid this trap and the disbelievers are encouraged to wake up before it is too late.

This verse could also be understood to mean that the mutual rivalry and accumulation of wealth diverts man to such a degree that they even go to the graveyards and boast about who their dead relatives were and what they did. They compete with each other in building structures over the graves of their ancestors and forget themselves.

This diversion has become so powerful that even the graveyards do not remind them of their impending death.

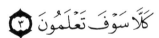 كَلَّا سَوْفَ تَعْلَمُونَ ٣

3. But you will soon know

Here Allaah gives us a severe warning against wasting our lives in the useless accumulation of material things and mutual boasting by hinting to us that we will soon know, without actually saying what, when and where. He tells us that this life is very short and we will soon realize just how foolish we were when we are finally lowered into our graves

---

[75] Collected by al-Bukhaaree (*Sahih al-Bukhari* (Arabic-English), vol.8, pp.296-297, nos. 444 & 446) and Muslim (*Sahih Muslim* (English Trans.), vol.2, p.415, no.3413).

and are confronted with its punishments and torments. On that day it will become very clear to us that all our boasting and hoarding was all in vain, as it was not what this life was really about. To illustrate the closeness of the next life, the Prophet (ﷺ) compared it to the shoes on our feet. 'Abdullaah quoted the Prophet (ﷺ) as saying, *"Paradise is nearer to each of you than the strap of his sandal, and so is the fire."*[76]

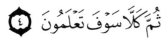

4. Then after that you will soon know.

The previous verse is dramatically repeated to increase its impact in the minds of the listeners. It also points to another time, shortly after the first encounter with the realities of death, when the follies of this life will seem even more tragic. We will be brought back to life to face the final judgement in which only righteous deeds will be of any avail.

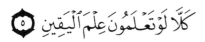

5. If only you had certain knowledge

Allaah adds another warning by assuring us that if we really knew just where we were headed, we would not allow our desires for wealth and fame divert us from our real purpose even for a minute. We would be so busy doing righteous deeds and avoiding evil deeds that we would not have any time to even think about hoarding money and boasting. This is why the Prophet (ﷺ), who had certain knowledge, was reported to have said, *"If you knew what I know, you would laugh little and cry a lot."*[77]

This verse has been purposely left incomplete by Allaah to increase its impact, by allowing the listener or reader to complete it in his own mind. This is considered, according to Arabic grammar, the height of eloquence.

---

[76]   Collected by al-Bukhaaree (*Sahih al-Bukhari* (Arabic-English), vol.8, p.326, no.492).
[77]   Collected by al-Bukhaaree (*Sahih al-Bukhari* (Arabic-English), vol.8. pp. 328-329, no.495).

6. You will surely see[78] the fire

This verse is also introduced by a particularly deleted oath to increase the certainty of its subject matter. The complete oath is: "By Allaah, you will see the fire." Everyone will be shown the Hellfire according to Allaah's statement:

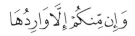

"There is none among you who won't be brought near to it (the Hellfire)."

Soorah Maryam (19) : 71

Its heartrending ferocity will shock the righteous, then they will be overcome with joy and gratitude in the knowledge that they will escape its flames by Allaah's mercy. But for the evil, the initial shock will only increase in intensity as it dawns on them that they are seeing their future eternal home. The Prophet (ﷺ) was quoted by Abu Hurayrah as saying, "*No one will enter Paradise without being shown the place he would have occupied in the fire if he had rejected faith, so that he would be more thankful. And no one will enter the fire without being shown the place he would have occupied in Paradise if he had accepted faith, so that he would be more sorrowful.*"[79] Abu Sa'eed al-Khudree related that the Prophet (ﷺ) said, concerning the Day of Judgement, " *...A bridge will be brought and placed over Hell.*" The companions asked, "*O Messenger of Allaah, what is the bridge?*" He replied, "*It is slippery and has hooks... some of the believers will cross the bridge in the blinking of an eye, others as quick as lightning, or a strong wind, fast horses or she-camels. Some will cross safely without any harm, other*

---

[78] *Note on Recitation*: Al-Kisaa'ee and Ibn 'Aamer read "*latarawunna*" according to the other recitation of the Prophet (ﷺ) as "*laturawunna*," which means "you will be shown."

[79] Collected by al-Bukhaaree (*Sahih al-Bukhari* (Arabic-English), vol.8, pp.372-373, no.573.

will receive some scratches and some will fall down into Hell. The last person will cross as if he were dragged over."[80]

7. Then you will really see it with certainty

The sinners will then be brought very close to the Fire to get an even more hair-raising view. The certainty of their entrance will be burned into their minds as they stand shaking in fear at its very edge.

Aynul-yageen is considered the highest level of knowledge about anything since no matter how detailed a description may be, it can never be equal to seeing a thing with one's own eyes.

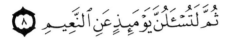

8. Then, verily you will be asked on that day about the pleasures.

On the Day of Judgement (*Qiyaamah*), everyone will be questioned about the blessings of ease, comfort and pleasure which Allaah gave them in this life as a test. Did we give the thanks which were due? Our wealth and children came to us with virtually no effort on our part. Even if it seems to us that things happen as a direct result of our efforts, if we look around us, we will see many people who made more effort than us, but got less, and others who made less efforts than us, but got more. Therefore, it wasn't our effort by itself which determined what we got in this life, it was only Allaah's mercy. Did we thank Him by remembering Him and obeying His commands, or were we ungrateful, forgetful and neglectful? That is the question around which the whole of man's life turns. This short life is only a test made up of that one fateful question, and its answer will determine our place in the next eternal life. Out of everything in this world, only our good deeds will be of any use to us in the next. Anas ibn Maalik reported that the Prophet (ﷺ) said, *"A dead person is followed by three, two of them return and*

---

[80] Collected by al-Bukhaaree (*Sahih al-Bukhari* (Arabic -English), vol.9, pp.395-399, no.532 (B)).

one remains: His relatives, his property and his deeds follow him; The relatives and property return and his deeds remain with him." [81]

The blessings Allaah has granted to us should be put to their right use. This is a means of expressing gratitude to Him. For instance, if we are in health, it can be used for the service of others; with wealth, the less fortunate can be helped; if we have knowledge, it can be passed on to others. We have not been sent on earth for eternity and hence, all the blessings given to us are only a means to achieve a worthwhile end, which is seeking Allaah's pleasure. Ibn 'Abbaas quoted the Prophet (ﷺ) as saying, "*There are two blessings of which many people are cheated: health and free time.*"[82]

These blessings are opportunities to do good which most people miss. Ibn 'Abbaas also reported that Allaah's Messenger (ﷺ) advised a man saying, '*Avail yourself of five things before five: your life before you die, your health before you become sick, your free time before you become busy, your youth before you become old, your wealth before you become poor.*" [83]

---

[81]   Collected by al-Bukhaaree (*Sahih al-Bukhari* (Arabic-English), vol.8, p. 343, no.521).

[82]   Collected by al-Bukhaaree (*Sahih al-Bukhari* (Arabic-English), vol.8, p. 282, no.421).

[83]   Collected by al-Haakim in *al-Mustadrak* and al-Bayhaqee in *Shu'ab al-Eemaan* and authenticated by al-Albaanee in *Saheeh al-Jaami' as-Sagheer* (1st ed.1969), vol.1, p.355, no.1088. The English text can be found in *al-Hadis*, vol.2, p.738, no.8, though the narration of this tradition from 'Amr ibn Maymoon was incomplete (*Mursal*).

QUESTIONS

1. The name *Takaathur* refers to
    (a) the accumulation of good deeds in this life for the next life to come.
    (b) the gathering of wealth, children and fame by the true believers in Allaah.
    (c) the test and trials which separate believers from disbelievers.
    (d) the diversion of people when they visit the graveyards.
    (e) the busy collection of this life's pleasures.

2. Verse 2: "**Until you visit the graves**." "You" in this verse refers to
    (a) the believers who visit the graves of their friends.
    (b) those people who have done many good deeds.
    (c) people who have been fooled by the accumulation of righteousness.
    (d) those whose love of this world's pleasures have made them forget death.
    (e) disbelievers who visit the homes of dead Muslims.

3. Visiting the graves could have either of the following two meanings:
    (a) actually going to the graveyards and going to the homes of dying people.
    (b) dying and being lowered into the grave and being buried alive.
    (c) being buried alive and visiting the graves of others to remember death.
    (d) going to the homes of dying people and being buried alive by one's friends.
    (e) dying and being buried, and visiting the graves of others.

4. According to this Soorah, until the graves are visited
    (a) people continue to die and be buried.
    (b) some people do many good deeds and collect rewards for themselves.
    (c) the graveyards are visited by people who boast about the tombstones of their relatives.
    (d) many people continue to blindly gather the pleasures of this life.

(e) people will be questioned about the pleasures of this life which Allaah gave them.

5. Verse 4: "**Then after that you will soon know**." It will soon be known
    (a) that we all must die and be judged.
    (b) that boasting and hoarding was a useless waste of time.
    (c) how foolish the disbelievers were for accumulating good deeds.
    (d) why the disbelievers have to die.
    (e) that boasting and hoarding was what life was all about.

6. Verse 4 is a repetition of verse 3
    (a) to emphasize the meaning of verse 3
    (b) to increase the impact in the minds of those lowered in the graves.
    (c) to make the meaning of verse 3 clear.
    (d) because the accumulation of wealth diverts true believers from their real purpose in life.
    (e) because those who visit the graveyards for the first time will know.

7. Verse 4 refers to
    (a) the time when one is lowered into the grave.
    (b) the Day of Judgement.
    (c) the time when those distracted by accumulation will be thrown into the fire.
    (d) when the disbelievers are about to die.
    (e) none of the above

8. In verse 4, "you" refers to
    (a) all of mankind.
    (b) true believers distracted by the accumulation of wealth in this life.
    (c) only the disbelievers in God.
    (d) those distracted by the accumulation of this world's pleasures.
    (e) those who are being lowered into their graves.

9. Verse 8: "**Then, you will be asked on that day about the pleasure.**" "you" in this verse refers to

    (a) all of mankind.

    (b) true believers distracted by the pleasures of this life.

    (c) only the disbelievers in God.

    (d) all who are distracted by the pleasures of this world.

    (e) none of the above.

10. Who will ask whom about what pleasures?

    (a) Prophet Muhammad (ﷺ) will ask his followers about the pleasures of this life.

    (b) Allaah will ask only the disbelievers about the blessings of ease and comfort which He gave them in this life.

    (c) The Prophets will ask all of their followers about the wealth and pleasures they gained from following the religion of Allaah.

    (d) Allaah will ask all mankind about the blessings they received in this life.

    (e) Allaah will ask only those diverted by the pleasures of this life about how they used them.

8. USOOL AL-HADEETH: THE ORIGIN OF THE SANAD

Teaching the Sunnah: The Era of the Prophet (ﷺ)

Anything which the Prophet of Islaam (ﷺ) said or did is considered to be a part of his *Sunnah* (i.e. way), which represents the practical application of Islaam according to divine guidance.

The Prophet (ﷺ) used to encourage his *Sahaabah*[84] to learn and memorize his *Sunnah* in many different ways. Sometimes he would sit them down and have them repeat after him certain *Du'aas*[85] which he wanted them to memorize, the same way he would have them learn the Qur'aan. On other occasions he would repeat himself three times so that they could memorize his more significant statements. Sometimes he would perform certain rites, then he would tell them to do it as he had done it. At other times, he would have some of the *Sahaabah* record in writing some more complicated things.

The Era of the Sahaabah

After the death of the Prophet (ﷺ), he older *Sahaabah* began to teach the younger *Sahaabah* the sayings and practices of the Prophet (ﷺ) which they had not been around to hear or observe. Both the younger and the older *Sahaabah* used to teach those who had accepted Islaam during the last days of the Prophet's (ﷺ) life, and thus never had an opportunity to learn anything directly from the Prophet (ﷺ).

When Islaam spread all over Arabia and into Syria, Iraq, Persia and Egypt during the reign of the Righteous Caliphs, the *Sahaabah* began to teach those who newly entered Islaam the principles of the religion. They would say to those who gathered around them, " I saw the Prophet do this," or "I heard the Prophet say that." This was how the chain of narration of the *Sunnah* began. Those new Muslims who studied under the *Sahaabah* were later referred to as the *Taabi'oon*.

---

[84] Anyone who saw Prophet Muhammad (ﷺ) and died in a state of Islaam is called a *Sahaabee* (pl. *Sahaabah*), meaning a companion, even if he was a child.
[85] Informal prayers.

Most of the *Taabi'oon* used to memorize the statements of the Prophet (ﷺ) which the <u>S</u>a<u>h</u>aabah used to quote. However, some of them also recorded the Prophet's *Sunnah* in writing. They used to travel to different parts of the Muslim world of that time in order to learn as much of the *Sunnah* of the Prophet (ﷺ) from as many of the <u>S</u>a<u>h</u>aabah as possible.

Why All This Effort?

It is natural that people try to watch and remember the sayings and deeds of anyone who is dear to them, and there is no doubt that Prophet Mu<u>h</u>ammad (ﷺ) was the most beloved person on earth to his followers. The Prophet (ﷺ) himself had enjoined this love on his community saying, *"None of you has truly believed until I become more dear to him than this son, his father and all of mankind."*[86]

Allaah, in the Qur'aan, emphasized for the whole of the Muslim *Ummah* the extreme importance of the *Sunnah* of the Prophet (ﷺ) by ordering them to obey all of his commands:

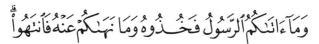

"Whatever the Messenger gives you, take it; and whatever he forbids you, leave it."

Soorah al-<u>H</u>ashr (59) : 7

How could the *Ummah* obey this divine command after the Prophet's death? How could they know what Allaah's Messenger (ﷺ) had commanded and forbidden if he was no longer with them? Therefore, great care had to be taken to preserve the *Sunnah* and convey it to each successive generation of Muslims. The Prophet (ﷺ) also stressed the great importance of passing on the *Sunnah* without any alterations by promising them Allaah's blessings saying, *"Allaah blesses any man who hears a saying of mine, memorizes it and understands it, then conveys just as he heard it; for perhaps one who is informed has more understanding*

---

[86] Collected by al-Bukhaaree (*Sa<u>h</u>i<u>h</u> al-Bukhari* (Arabic-English), vol.1, p.20, no.14) and Muslim (*Sa<u>h</u>i<u>h</u> Muslim* (English Trans.), vol.1, p.31, no.70).

than the one who heard it." [87] He also stressed it by warning them of the severe punishment awaiting anyone who lies on him saying *"Whoever lies on me will find his seat in the Hellfire!"*[88]

The Era of the Taabi'oon

When the <u>Sah</u>aabah began to die out and Islaam spread into India, Afghanistan, Russia, China, North Africa and Spain, the *Taabi'oon* took up where the <u>Sah</u>aabah had left off and began the great task of teaching the new converts to Islaam the principles of the religion. They would say to those who gathered around them, " I heard such and such a <u>Sah</u>aabee say that he saw the Prophet (ﷺ) do this," or, " I heard such and such a <u>Sah</u>aabee say that he heard the Prophet (ﷺ) say that." In this way the second link in the chain of narration of the *Sunnah* was added.

Those who studied under the *Taabi'oon* were later called *Atbaa' at-Taabi'een* (followers of the followers). Many of these new students used to travel for days or even months to meet and study under various *Taabe'oon*, taking great care in the memorization and the writing down of their teacher's narrations.

During this period, the righteous caliph, 'Umar ibn 'Abdul 'Azeez, commanded all the great scholars of that time to collect all the statements and actions of the Prophet (ﷺ) which were being taught because some people in Iraq had begun to make up stories about the Prophet (ﷺ). One of the first scholars among the *Taabi'oon* to record the narrations about the Prophet (ﷺ) was Mu<u>h</u>ammad ibn Muslim ibn Shihaab az-Zuhree. Ibn Shihaab not only recorded the statements, but also the names of the narrators and information about them so that those who were making up <u>H</u>adeeths could be easily identified.

---

[87] Collected by Aboo Daawood (*Sunan Abu Dawud* (English Trans.), vol.3, p.1038, no.3652) and at-Tirmi<u>th</u>ee and authenticated by al-Albaanee in *Saheeh Sunan Abee Daawood*, vol.2, p. 697, no.3108).

[88] Reported by az-Zubayr ibn 'Awwaam and collected by al-Bukhaaree (<u>Sah</u>ih al-Bukhari (Arabic-English), vol.1, p.83, nos. 107-109), Muslim (<u>Sah</u>ih Muslim), vol.4, p.1543, no.7147) and Abu Daawood (*Sunan Abu Dawud* (English Trans.), vol.3, p.1036, no.3643.

Even though the process of writing down _Hadeeths_ had begun on a large scale, the oral transmission of _Hadeeths_ continued because much more could be conveyed in a shorter period of time. Writing was a slow and tedious process in those days. Writing materials were scare and the printing press had not been invented.

So the _Atbaa' at-Taabi'een_ taught those who gathered around them much in the same way in which they were taught themselves. They would say to their students, "I heard such and such a _Taabi'ee_ say that he heard such and such a _Sahaabee_ say that he saw the Prophet (ﷺ) do this," or " I heard such and such a _Taabi'ee_ say that he heard such and such a _Sahaabee_ say that he heard the Prophet (ﷺ) say that." Only a few books of _Hadeeth_ from the time of the _Atbaa' at-Taabi'een_ have reached us. The most famous of them is the book of Maalik ibn Anas called _Al-Muwatta_, and the most famous copy of _Al-Muwatta_ is that of Maalik's student Yahyaa ibn Yahyaa from the Berber tribe of Masmoodah.

In the second volume of Yahyaa's copy of _Al-Muwatta_, in the chapter on the _Dabb_ (lizard), we find the following: "_Maalik told me from Ibn Shihaab from Abu Umaamah ibn Sahl (ibn Hurayf) from 'Abdullaah ibn 'Abbaas from Khaalid ibn al-Waleed that he accompanied the Prophet (ﷺ) to his wife Maymoonah's house and a roasted **Dabb** was brought for him (to eat)... so Allaah's Messenger stretched out his hand to eat some of it. Some of the women who were with Maymoonah said, 'Inform Allaah's Messenger of what he is about to eat.' When he was told that it was **Dabb**, he removed his hand from it and (Khaalid ibn al-Waleed) asked, 'Is it Haraam, O Messenger of Allaah?' He replied, 'No, but it wasn't in my people's land and I find it loathsome.' Khaalid then said, 'I then tore off (a piece of) it and ate it while the Prophet (ﷺ) watched me.'_" [89]

The _Sanad_ (chain of transmission) of this _Hadeeth_ is as follows:

---

[89] Collected by Maalik (_Muwatta Imam Maalik_ (English Trans.), p. 410, no.1745).

Prophet (ﷺ) <<<

Sahaabah
Khaalid <<< Ibn Abbaas <<< Abu Umaamah <<<

Taabi'oon
Ibn Shihaab <<<

Atbaa' at-Taabi'een
Maalik <<<

Atbaa' atbaa' at-Taabi'een
Yahyaa

Khaalid ibn al-Waleed, Ibn 'Abbaas and Abu Umaamah were all *Sahaabah*, but Ibn 'Abbaas was a young *Sahaabee* and Abu Umaamah only saw the Prophet (ﷺ) just before his death. So Khaalid related this incident to Ibn 'Abbaas when he asked him about eating *Dabb* and Ibn 'Abbaas related it to Abu Umaamah who then told Ibn Shihaab who told Maalik, who in turn wrote it down and told Yahyaa.

Following that *Hadeeth* is another narration on the same topic: "*Maalik informed me from 'Abdullaah ibn Deenar from Ibn 'Umar that a man called out to the Prophet of Allaah, 'O Prophet of Allaah, what do you say about **Dabb**?' The Prophet of Allaah replied, 'I don't eat it and I don't forbid it.*"[90]

In this case the *Sanad* is shorter because the *Sahaabee* Ibn 'Umar related it directly to his student Ibn Deenar.

Prophet (ﷺ) >>>

Sahaabah
Ibn Umar >>>

Taabi'oon
Ibn Deenar >>>

Atbaa' at-Taabi'een
Maalik >>>

Atbaa' atbaa' at-Taabi'een
Yahyaa

---

[90] Collected by Maalik (*Muwatta Imam Maalik* (English Trans.), p.411, no.1746).

QUESTIONS

1. A Sahaabee is
   (a) anyone who saw the Prophet (ﷺ) after the *Hijrah*.
   (b) any Muslim over the age of puberty who saw the Prophet (ﷺ).
   (c) anyone who lived in the time of the Prophet (ﷺ) and died in a state of Islaam.
   (d) someone who saw the Prophet's companions and died in a state of Islaam.
   (e) one who saw the Prophet (ﷺ) and died a Muslim.

2. The Prophet (ﷺ) encouraged his companions to learn his *Sunnah* by
   (a) writing it down for them.
   (b) making them write down everything that he said and did.
   (c) having them repeat everything that he said.
   (d) repeating himself three times so that they could memorize his more significant statements.
   (e) giving a practical demonstration of everything he told them to do or not do.

3. The first link in the *Sanad* of *Hadeeths* was formed
   (a) when the *Taabi'oon* taught old Muslims and other *Sahaabah* who were not familiar with the Prophet's *Sunnah*.
   (b) when the *Sahaabah* fought the Christians and Jews who were not familiar with Islaam.
   (c) when the Prophet (ﷺ) taught the Muslims and the *Sahaabah* who were unfamiliar with his *Sunnah*.
   (d) when the *Sahaabah* who were not familiar with the Prophet's *Sunnah*.
   (e) when the *Sahaabah* who were unfamiliar with the Prophet's *Sunnah* taught new Muslims the practices of old Muslims.

4. The order to collect in writing the Hadeeths of the Prophet (ﷺ) was given by 'Umar ibn 'Abdul 'Azeez because
   (a) the *Sahaabah* had begun to forget the *Sunnah* of the Prophet (ﷺ).
   (b) he wanted to study the Prophet's *Sunnah* in order to be a good

caliph.

(c) the great scholars of his time had begun to forget some of the *Hadeeths* which they learned from the *Sahaabah*.

(d) some scholars had begun to make up stories about the Prophet (ﷺ).

(e) none of the above.

5. The earliest book of *Hadeeth* to reach us and its author are

   (a) *al-Muwatta* by Yahyaa ibn Yahyaa.

   (b) *Saheeh al-Bukhaaree* by Muhammad ibn Ismaa'eel al-Bukhaaree.

   (c) *ad-Dabb* by 'Abdullaah ibn 'Abbaas.

   (d) *al-Maalik* by Muwatta ibn Anas.

   (e) *al-Muwatta* by Maalik ibn Anas.

6. Al-Bukhaaree is most noted as being

   (a) the *Sahaabee* who narrated the most *Hadeeths*.

   (b) the compiler of the most accurate book of *Hadeeth*, called *al-Muwatta*.

   (c) writer of the first book of *Hadeeth*, called *Saheeh al-Bukhaaree*.

   (d) one of the most accurate books of *Hadeeths*.

9. HADEETH ONE: THE COMEDIAN

عَنْ بَهْزِ بْنِ حَكِيمٍ قَالَ حَدَّثَنِي أَبِي عَنْ أَبِيهِ قَالَ سَمِعْتُ رَسُولَ اللَّـهِ
صَلَّى اللَّهُ عَلَيْهِ وَسَلَّمَ يَقُولُ: ((وَيْلٌ لِلَّذِي يُحَدِّثُ فَيَكْذِبُ
لِيُضْحِكَ بِهِ الْقَوْمَ وَيْلٌ لَهُ وَيْلٌ لَهُ))

Bahz ibn Hakeem reported from his father who reported from his grandfather that Allaah's Messenger (ﷺ) said, "Woe be on the one who speaks and lies in order to make people laugh, woe be on him."
Collected by Abu Daawood[91] and at-Tirmithee

The Narrator

The name of Bahz's grandfather was Mu'aawiyah ibn Haydaah. He was a _Sahaabee_ from the tribe of Qushayr. He settled in Basrah during the military campaigns in Iraq, and later died in Khurasan.

The Collectors

Abu Daawood's actual name was Sulaymaan ibn al-Ash'ath. He was given the title as-Sijistaanee and he was born in Basrah in the year 202 A.H.(818 C.E.). He studied _Hadeeth_ under Imaam Ahmed along with al-Bukhaaree and taught many of the later scholars of _Hadeeth_, such as at-Tirmithee and an-Nasaa'ee.

Abu Daawood selected 4,800 _Hadeeths_ from over 500,000 which he had gathered, and organized them in a book which he named _Sunan_ [plural of _Sunnah_, which means a practice of the Prophet (ﷺ)]. Abu Daawood taught his _Sunan_ in Baghdaad and other major centers of Islaam of that time. He died in Basrah in the year 275 A.H. (889 C.E.).

---

[91] _Sunan Abu Dawud_ (English Trans.) , vol.3, p.1389, no. 4972 and authenticated by al-Albaanee in _Saheeh Sunan Abee Daawood_, vol.3, p.492, no.4175.

The *Sunan* of Abu Daawood was translated into English by Aḥmad Hasaan in 1979, however it was first published in three volumes by Sh. Muḥammad Ashraf Publishers in 1984 in Pakistan.

The full name of at-Tirmithee was Muḥammad ibn 'Eesaa ibn Surah. He was born in Tirmith and studied *Hadeeth* under al-Bukhaaree and Abu Daawood, as well as other teachers. He composed a book of *Hadeeth* which he called *Al-Jaami'*, but which later became known as *As-Sunan*. He contributed a lot to the science of *Hadeeth* criticism and composed a book called *Al-Elaal* (The Defects) after he had become blind. At-Tirmithee dictated both his *Sunan* and *Al-'Elal* to students in al-Ḥijaz, al-Iraq and Khurasan. He died in Tirmith in the year 881 C.E. (267 A.H.).

GENERAL MEANING

Allaah commanded the believers to be truthful because true belief in Allaah obliges the believer to avoid lies. If we truly believed that Allaah sees and hears all that we do, could we then lie? To lie means to disbelieve that we will have to answer to Allaah for what we do. Thus, the more one lies, the weaker his faith gets, and the more one is truthful the stronger his faith gets. The Qur'aan says:

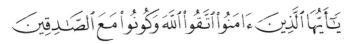

"O you who believe! Fear Allaah and be with those who are truthful."

Soorah at-Tawbah (9) : 119

Because of this and the Qur'anic commandments requiring the believers to be truthful, the Prophet (ﷺ) forbade all forms of lies on many occasions, for example, he was reported to have said, *"Beware of the lie, for surely lies lead to blasphemy and blasphemy leads to the Fire."*[92]

---

[92] Narrated by Ibn Mas'ood and collected by Muslim (*Sahih Muslim* (English Trans.), vol. 4, pp. 1375-1376, no.6309) and Abu Daawood (*Sunan Abu Dawud* (English Trans.), vol.3, p.1389, no.4971).

At other times he would discourage lying by describing some of the punishments awaiting liars. The Prophet (ﷺ) related to us a dream in which he saw people being punished in hell - and the dreams of the prophets were a form of revelation. He described one person in the fire whose cheek he saw being torn from his mouth to his ear. And he related that two men came to him during the dream and informed him that the person whose cheek was ripped open from ear to ear was one was told lies which become widespread.[93]

In this *Hadeeth*, the Prophet (ﷺ) decided to focus on a specific form of lying, telling jokes and exaggeration, because they are so common. It has even been referred to as a "white lie" in order to distinguish it from the intentional harmful lie, but the Prophet (ﷺ) forbade it even though its intention is only amusement and it does not contain any apparent harm. The reason for this is because the one who lies habitually for the sake of amusement loses the fear of lying and may later easily fall into harmful lies. The Prophet (ﷺ) blocked this path because of where it leads and because its value is negligible. This prohibition specifically refers to jokes about different races or cultures which lead to scorn and abuse, which Allaah has also forbidden in the Qur'aan:

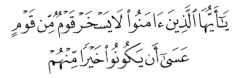

"O you who believe! A group of people should not scorn another group, for it may be that (the scorned group) is better than the other..."

Soorah al-Hujuraat (49) : 11

However, jokes which are free from exaggeration and abuse are permitted as long as the audience is aware that the stories are fictitious. The best types of jokes are those involving true incidents which happen every day to all of us.

---

[93] Collected by al-Bukhaaree (*Sahih al-Bukhari* (Arabic-English), vol.8, p. 76, no.118).

It is also forbidden to listen to lies without informing the liar of the seriousness of his or her act, as it is obligatory on every Muslim to order righteousness and forbid them from evil. Allaah said.

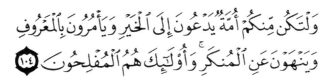

"Let there arise out of you a band of people inviting to all that is good, enjoining what is right, and forbidding what is wrong; They are the ones who will succeed."

Soorah Aal-'Imraan (3) : 104

Listening to jokes involving lies is forbidden because silence in Islaam indicates consent, and the Prophet (﷽) ordered us to stop evil or speak out against it if it occurs in our presence. If we are too shy or cannot muster the courage to speak up against the one who lies, then the least we can do is to leave the company of those who indulge in this sort of pastime.

Lessons

1. Lying to amuse others is forbidden in Islaam.
2. Listening to lies without speaking out is also forbidden.
3. Islaam is concerned about blocking all paths which lead to the *Haraam.*

QUESTIONS

1. Bahz ibn Hakeem was
   (a) the collector of the Hadeeth on lies.
   (b) the son of Mu'aawiyah ibn Haydaah.
   (c) a companion of the Prophet (ﷺ).
   (d) born in Basrah and died during a military campaign in southern Arabia.
   (e) the grandson of the Prophet's companion Mu'aawiyah ibn Haydaah.

2. Abu Daawood
   (a) was the teacher of Imaam Ahmad along with al-Bukhaaree.
   (b) collected *Hadeeths* of the Prophet (ﷺ) in a book which he called *Sunan*.
   (c) reported the *Hadeeth* on lies from his grandfather, Mu'aawiyah ibn Haydaah.
   (d) was one of the Prophet's companions.
   (e) was none of the above.

3. The actual name of Abu Daawood is
   (a) Daawood ibn Abu Sulaymaan as-Sijistaanee.
   (b) Sulaymaan ibn Daawood al-Ash'ath as-Sijistaanee.
   (c) Sulaymaan ibn al-Ash'ath.
   (d) Abu Daawood ibn Sulaymaan ibn al-Ash'ath as-Sijistaanee.
   (e) Sulaymaan as-Sijistaanee.

4.   (a) what was at-Tirmithee's full name and why was he called at-Tirmithee?
     (b) who were his two main teachers ?
     (c) what is *al-Jaami'*?

5. Islaam does not differentiate between "white lies" and serious or harmful lies because
    (a) neither type of lie is truly harmful except in rare cases.
    (b) telling "white lies" removes the seriousness from something that is very serious, thereby paving the way for one to tell lies that are harmful.
    (c) "white lies" can also be harmful if one get caught telling them.
    (d) a person who habitually tells serious lies can easily fall into habitually telling "white lies."
    (e) there is really no such thing as a "black lie."

6. If we do not have the courage or are too shy to speak out against lying
    (a) we should listen to what the liar is saying and make sure that we don't repeat it.
    (b) we should tell the lies to others while reminding them of the seriousness of lying.
    (c) we should at least leave the company of the one who is telling lies.
    (d) we should not pay attention to what the liar is saying.
    (e) we should not laugh at the jokes even if we find them funny.

7. Listening to amusing lies is forbidden if we do not speak out against it because
    (a) silence means consent in Islaam.
    (b) laughing means consent in Islaam.
    (c) listening means consent.
    (d) listening to lies is the same as telling lies
    (e) the sin of listening is greater than the sin of telling lies.

10. HADEETH TWO:
AVOIDING THE UNIMPORTANT

عَنْ أَبِي هُرَيْرَةَ قَالَ قَالَ رَسُولُ اللَّهِ صَلَّى اللَّهُ عَلَيْهِ وَسَلَّمَ:

((مِنْ حُسْنِ إِسْلَامِ الْمَرْءِ تَرْكُهُ مَا لاَ يَعْنِيهِ))

Abu Hurayrah said that Allaah's Messenger (ﷺ) said, "Among the things which complete a man's Islaam is leaving that which doesn't concern him."

Collected by at-Tirmi<u>th</u>ee[94]

The Narrator

Abu Hurayrah's full name was 'Abdur-Ra<u>h</u>maan ibn Sakhr. He was born in Yemen and came to Madeenah after the Hijrah[95] to accept Islaam from the Prophet (ﷺ) himself. The Prophet (ﷺ) nicknamed him Abu Hurayrah because he often used to carry a little kitten in his arms. Abu Hurayrah narrated 1,236 *Hadeeths*, which was more than any other *Sahaabee*. He died and was buried in Madeenah in the year 697 C.E, at the age of 78.

The Collector

At-Tirmi<u>th</u>ee's biography can be found in *Hadeeth* number one.

GENERAL MEANING

The Prophet (ﷺ), in this *Hadeeth*, gives us a priceless piece of guidance whose application raises a Muslim to the highest levels of Islaam. Many people often fall into *Haraam* by getting involved in things that don't really concern them. Curiosity has its place in science, as well as in day-to-day dealings, but it has to be kept under control, otherwise it

---

[94] Collected in *al-Hadis*, vol. 1, p.456, no.190 from 'Alee ibn Husayn and authenticated by al-Albaanee in *Sa<u>h</u>eeh Sunan at-Tirmi<u>th</u>ee*, vol.2, pp. 268-269, no.1886.
[95] The Prophet's emigration from Makkah to Madeenah.

could lead the curious into mischief. An example of this is peeking through keyholes to find out what is going on in places which are forbidden. The Prophet (ﷺ) dealt severely with this tendency by making the seeking of permission before entering foreign houses or buildings compulsory. He also allowed the one whose privacy had been invaded to cause bodily harm to the invader without fear of punishment saying, *"If a man sees you (naked) without your permission and you blinded him by throwing a stone in his eye, there would be no blame on you."*[96]

Nosey individuals who pry into other people's business and listen in on their private conversations have also allowed their curiosity to lead them into what was of no real concern to them, and thereby into *Haraam*. The Prophet (ﷺ) warned the eavesdroppers of an impending punishment for their uncontrolled curiosity saying, *"Whoever hears a people's conversation which they disliked him to hear, will have molten brass poured in his ears on the Day of Resurrection."*[97]

This *Hadeeth*, in effect, encourages us to seek the things which are of real value to us. That is, we should strive to find the righteous deeds which will help us in the next life and avoid the useless trivialities which are of no real value in either this life or the next. For instance, watching movies for hours or playing card games. We are accountable to Allaah for the way we spend our time, and the way we utilize time also shows where our priorities lie and whether our love of Allaah is above everything else as it needs to be. Allaah said,

قُلْ إِن كَانَ ءَابَآؤُكُمْ وَأَبْنَآؤُكُمْ وَإِخْوَٰنُكُمْ وَأَزْوَٰجُكُمْ وَعَشِيرَتُكُمْ وَأَمْوَٰلٌ ٱقْتَرَفْتُمُوهَا وَتِجَٰرَةٌ تَخْشَوْنَ كَسَادَهَا وَمَسَٰكِنُ تَرْضَوْنَهَآ أَحَبَّ إِلَيْكُم مِّنَ ٱللَّهِ وَرَسُولِهِۦ وَجِهَادٍ فِى سَبِيلِهِۦ فَتَرَبَّصُوا۟ حَتَّىٰ يَأْتِىَ ٱللَّهُ بِأَمْرِهِۦ

---

[96] Reported by Abu Hurayrah and collected by Muslim (*Sahih Muslim* (English Trans.), vol.3, p.1180, no.5371).

[97] Reported by Ibn 'Abbaas and collected by al-Bukhaaree (*Sahih al-Bukhari* (Arabic-English), vol.9, p. 134, no.165).

"Say: If your fathers, sons, brothers, wives, relatives; wealth you have earned; business in which you fear loss, and homes which you enjoy are more beloved to you than Allaah and His Messenger, and Jihaad, then wait until Allaah's command (for punishment) comes..."

Soorah at-Tawbah (9) : 24

وَمِنَ ٱلنَّاسِ مَن يَتَّخِذُ مِن دُونِ ٱللَّهِ أَندَادًا يُحِبُّونَهُمْ
كَحُبِّ ٱللَّهِ وَٱلَّذِينَ ءَامَنُوٓاْ أَشَدُّ حُبًّا لِّلَّهِ

"And among mankind are some who take others besides Allaah as rivals. They love them as they love Allaah. But the believers love Allaah more (than anything else)..."

Soorah al-Baqarah (2) : 165

In avoiding things which are of no real importance, we provide ourselves a lot of time in which to do constructive things. We also conserve our energies by saving them from being wasted on things of no value, thereby giving us an added supply which could be used in areas of value.

Lessons

1. Avoiding the unimportant is among the greatest virtues in Islaam.
2. Being concerned about that which is of no concern can easily lead to _Haraam_.
3. A Muslim should seek things of real importance (righteous deeds).

QUESTIONS

1. Abu Hurayrah's real name was
    (a) Sakhr ibn 'Abdur-Rahmaan.
    (b) Abu Rahmaan ibn Sakhr.
    (c) Hurayrah ibn Sakhr.
    (d) 'Abdur-Rahmaan ibn Sakhr.
    (e) given to him by Prophet Muhammad (ﷺ).

2. He was named Abu Hurayrah by
    (a) his father.
    (b) the Prophet (ﷺ).
    (c) his cat.
    (d) his tribe.
    (e) 'Abdur-Rahmaan.

3. Abu Hurayrah was most famous for
    (a) his compilation of *Hadeeths* called *Sunan Abee Hurayrah*.
    (b) the largest compilation of *Hadeeths* called *al-Musnad*.
    (c) narrating more *Hadeeths* than any other companion of the Prophet (ﷺ).
    (d) being the teacher of Abu Daawood, along with al-Bukhaaree.
    (e) his extraordinary kindness to animals.

4. The *Hadeeth*, "*Among the things which complete a man's Islaam is leaving that which doesn't concern him*" means
    (a) a person who pries into others affairs is really a disbeliever.
    (b) we should not ask others about themselves.
    (c) we should strive to eliminate curiosity from ourselves.
    (d) we should keep our curiosity under control so that we will avoid wrong-doing.

5. Why did the Prophet (ﷺ) make asking permission to enter foreign houses and buildings compulsory?

6.Listening in on people's private conversations without their permission is

    (a) forbidden

    (b) allowable if one fears that the people are talking about him.

    (c) allowable if you know the people, but forbidden if you do not know them.

    (d) not recommended because one might misunderstand what is being said.

    (e) allowable as long as you do not repeat what you have heard.

7. Explain how this *Hadeeth* encourages us to seek out things that are of real value.

11. HADEETH THREE: INNOVATIONS

عَنْ عَائِشَةَ رَضِيَ اللهُ عَنْهَا قَالَتْ قَالَ رَسُولُ اللهِ صَلَّى اللهُ عَلَيْهِ :

((مَنْ أَحْدَثَ فِي أَمْرِنَا هَذَا مَا لَيْسَ فِيهِ فَهُوَ رَدٌّ))

'Aa'eshah reported that Allaah's Messenger (ﷺ) said, "Whoever innovates in this affair of ours something which doesn't belong in it will be rejected."

Collected by al-Bukhaaree and Muslim[98]

The Narrator

'Aa'eshah bint Abee Bakr was the third wife of the Prophet (ﷺ). She was considered a great scholar of Islaam and many students used to come and study under her after the death of the Prophet (ﷺ). 'Aa'eshah is also among those who related the most *Hadeeths* of the Prophet (ﷺ). Her death was in the year 57 *Hijrah* (679 C.E.), and she was buried in Madeenah.

The Collectors

Al-Bukhaaree's name at the time of his birth in 810 C.E. was Muhammad ibn Ismaa'eel. He was called al-Bukhaaree because he was born in the city of Bukhaaraa, which is now in the state of Uzbekistan. Imaam Bukhaaree began his study of *Hadeeth* from the early age of 10. His father Ismaa'eel was himself a scholar or *Hadeeth* who had studied the subject under some very famous scholars, such as Maalik ibn Anas and Hammaad ibn Zayd. Al-Bukhaaree travelled all over the Muslim world collecting *Hadeeths* and composed his famous collection of *Hadeeths*, which he called *al-Jaami' as-Saheeh al-Musnad*, but which later became known as *Saheeh al-Bukhaaree*. *Saheeh al-Bukhaaree* contained 2,602 *Hadeeths* which he chose from the many thousands that he had memorized.

---

[98] *Sahih al-Bukhari* (Arabic-English), vol.3, p. 535, no.861, and *Sahih Muslim* (English Trans.), vol.3, p.931, no.4266. Also collected by Abu Daawood (*Sunan Abu Dawud* (English Trans.), vol.3, p.1294, no.4598.

Al-Bukhaaree died in Samarkand, the present-day capital of Uzbekistan, in the year 870 C.E. at the age of 60.

Saheeh al-Bukhaaree is considered by Muslim scholars to be the most authentic book in Islaam after the Qur'aan. *Saheeh al-Bukhaaree* has been translated into English by Muhammad Muhsin Khan and was published in 1976 by the Islamic University of Madeenah.

Muslim's full name was Muslim ibn al-Hajjaj al-Qushayree. He was born in 817 C.E. in the city of Nishapur which is in the north eastern part of Iran near the city of Meshed. Muslim began his study of *Hadeeth* at the age of 15 and travelled to Iraq, Hijaaz (the western coast of Arabia), Syria and Egypt in order to study under great scholars of *Hadeeth* like *al-Bukhaaree*, Ahmad ibn Hanbal, 'Abdullaah ibn Humayd and Ibn Abee Shaybah. He later had many students who went on to become great scholars after his death. Among the most famous of his students were at-Tirmithee and Ibn Abee Haatim.

Muslim compiled a *Hadeeth* book containing 3,000 *Hadeeths* which he called *al-Jaami' as -Saheeh*, but which later became known as *Saheeh Muslim*. *Saheeh Muslim* is considered by most Muslim scholars to be the most accurate book of *Hadeeth* after that of al-Bukhaaree. It has been translated into English by Abdul Hamid Siddiqui and was published in four volumes in Pakistan in 1976.

Imaam Muslim died in the city of his birth in the year 875 C.E. at the age of 58, but left to all the generations of Muslims who came after him a great contribution.

GENERAL MEANING

The Prophet (ﷺ) warned us not to make up any new things and then call them a part of Islaam. Islaam is what the Prophet (ﷺ) brought for us to follow. If we fabricate any new practices, they will be rejected by Allaah, as he told us,

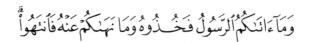

"Take what the Messenger has given you and avoid what he has forbidden."

Soorah al-Hashr (59) : 7

Therefore, we should make sure that all we do in the name of Islaam is from the Prophet of Islaam (ﷺ) and not from our various cultures. An example of this is how some people celebrate the Prophet's birthday just as Christians celebrate the birthday of Jesus (may Allaah's peace be on him) even though the Prophet (ﷺ) never said we should do so and none of his *Sahaabah* did so. In fact, we do not even know the exact date on which the Prophet (ﷺ) was born. The Prophet (ﷺ) also informed us that we have only two yearly *'Eids* (celebrations), which are *'Eid al-Fitr* and *'Eid al-Ad-haa*. Anas reported that when the Prophet (ﷺ) came to Madeenah, there were two days in which they would celebrate. When he asked about the origin of the two festivals, they replied that they used to play on those days in the pre-Islamic period. The Prophet (ﷺ) said, *"Allaah has exchanged them with better things for you: the 'Eed of sacrifice and the 'Eed of breaking the fast."*[99]

Some Muslims today kiss and rub everything of religious value believing that it will bring them blessings and good fortune. They kiss and rub the Qur'aan, their *Thikr* beads (which are another innovation), the pillars of the Prophet's *Masjid*, and many other things, yet the only thing of religious significance which the Prophet (ﷺ) kissed or touched was the black stone on the corner of the *Ka'bah*.

Allaah said in the Qur'aan,

$$ ٱلْيَوْمَ أَكْمَلْتُ لَكُمْ دِينَكُمْ $$

"This day I have completed your religion for you."

Soorah al-Maa'idah (5) : 3

---

[99] Collected by Abu Daawood (*Sunan Abu Dawud* (English-Trans.), vol.1, p.293, no.1130. See also *al-Hadis*, vol.3, p.479, no.728. This *Hadeeth* was authenticated in *Saheeh Sunan Abee Daawood*, vol.1, p.210, no.1004.

When we make up new things we are really saying that the religion of Islaam was not completed and the Prophet (ﷺ) did not know what was best for us.

Lessons

1. We should reject all innovations which go against the laws of Islaam.
2. We should take care to follow the Prophet (ﷺ) closely and avoid innovations.
3. Whatever is found in the laws of Islaam should be accepted and followed.

QUESTIONS

1. Give three points about the narrator of this *Hadeeth*.

2. Al-Bukhaaree's actual name was
    (a) Muhammad ibn Ismaa'eel al-Qushayree.
    (b) Ismaa'eel ibn Muhammad al-Bukhaaree.
    (c) Muhammad ibn al-Hajjaaj.
    (d) Muhammad ibn Ismaa'eel.
    (e) Ismaa'eel ibn Muhammad.

3. He was called al-Bukhaaree because.
    (a) he was born in the city of Bukhaaraa.
    (b) he named his compilation of *Hadeeths* "*Saheeh* al-Bukhaaree."
    (c) that was the name of his father.
    (d) it is the name of the city in which he died.
    (e) the Prophet (ﷺ) nicknamed him by that name.

4. Al-Bukhaaree was famous for
    (a) narrating more *Hadeeths* of the Prophet (ﷺ) than any other companion.
    (b) gathering the largest collection of *Hadeeths*, which he called *Saheeh al-Bukhaaree*.
    (c) compiling the most authentic book of *Hadeeths*.
    (d) being the founder of one of the four schools of Islamic law.
    (e) writing the most authentic commentary on the Qur'aan.

5. Muslim was called "Muslim" because
    (a) that was the name of the town in which he was born.
    (b) he was a convert to Islaam.
    (c) that was his given name.
    (d) it was the name of his father.
    (e) he was known to be a good Muslim.

6. Muslim named his collection of _Hadeeths_
    (a) _Saheeh Muslim._
    (b) _al-Muslim as-_ _Saheeh._
    (c) _al-Musnad as-_ _Saheeh._
    (d) _al-Jaami'as-_ _Saheeh_ _al-Musnad._
    (e) _al-Jaami' Muslim._

7. This _Hadeeth_ teaches us to
    (a) be backward and not make any new inventions.
    (b) avoid doing new things in our day-to-day lives.
    (c) be inventive in order to earn Allaah's blessings.
    (d) not invent new practices in Islaam.
    (e) avoid anything new which we find in _Hadeeths._

8. From this _Hadeeth_ we learn that the practice of celebrating the Prophet's birthday and kissing the Qur'aan are considered
    (a) recommended, because they are both good innovations.
    (b) disliked, because the _Sahaabah_ only rarely did them.
    (c) forbidden, since the Prophet (ﷺ) never did them, nor did his companions.
    (d) recommended, as the Prophet (ﷺ) advised us to do so.
    (e) _Haraam_, since the Prophet (ﷺ) told us not to celebrate his birthday and not to kiss the Qur'aan

9. Celebrating one's own birthday is also
    (a) forbidden, as the Prophet (ﷺ) said it was _Haraam._
    (b) disliked, since the _Sahaabah_ used to discourage it.
    (c) allowed, because the Prophet (ﷺ) used to celebrate his.
    (d) forbidden, as it is an innovation in religion.
    (e) disliked, since it is an imitation of non-Muslim practices.

10. The meaning of the phrase _"this affair of ours"_ in the _Hadeeth is_
    (a) our day-to-day affairs.
    (b) life in general.
    (c) Islaam.
    (d) the Prophet's birthday.
    (e) none of the above.

12. HADEETH FOUR:
ISLAM IN THEORY AND PRACTICE

عَنِ ابْنِ عَبَّاسٍ قَالَ قَالَ رَسُولُ اللّهِ صَلَّى اللّهُ عَلَيْهِ وَسَلَّمَ:

((لَيَقْرَأَنَّ الْقُرْآنَ نَاسٌ مِنْ أُمَّتِي يَمْرُقُونَ مِـنَ الْإِسْـلاَمِ كَمَا

يَمْرُقُ السَّهْمُ مِنَ الرَّمِيَّةِ))

Ibn 'Abbaas reported that Allaah's Messenger (ﷺ) said, "There will surely be a people from my *Ummah* who will recite the Qur'aan, but they will fly out of Islaam as (easily) as an arrow passes through its target."

Collected by Aḥmad and Ibn Maajah[100]

The Narrator

'Abdullaah ibn 'Abbaas was born in Makkah around 619 C.E. and was a cousin of the Prophet (ﷺ). He later became one of the greatest legal scholars among the *Saḥaabah*. The Prophet (ﷺ) himself called him "*Turjumaan al-Qur'aan*,"[101] the most able commentator of the Qur'aan.[102] He was also among those who reported a large number of *Hadeeth*. He died in the city of Ṯaa'if in the year 68 A.H. (691 C.E.) at the age of 72.

The Collector

Aḥmad Ibn Hambal (died 855 C.E.) was among the great collectors of *Hadeeth*. He named his collection *al-Musnad*, but it came to be known as *Musnad Aḥmad*. It was the largest collection of *Hadeeths* among the early books and contained over 40,000 *Hadeeths*. His collection was arranged according to the names of the Prophet's companions who nar-

---

[100] Authenticated by al-Albaanee in *Saheeh al-Jaami' aṣ-Ṣagheer*, vol. 5, p.106, no.5339.
[101] Literally, translator of the Qur'aan.
[102] Collected by al-Bukhaaree (*Sahih al-Bukhari* (Arabic-English), vol.1, p.64, no.75, and vol.5, p.69, nos. 100 & 101.

rated traditions from the Prophet (ﷺ). Ahmad also became one of the four most notable legal scholars, commonly called the four *Imaams* and he founded the school of Islamic law called the *Hambalee Math-hab*. This school is now followed mainly in Saudi Arabia.

GENERAL MEANING

Allaah's Messenger (ﷺ) informs us in this *Hadeeth* that there will be among the nation of Islaam people who will call themselves Muslims and recite the Qur'aan beautifully, but leave Islaam and work against its followers at the first opportunity that they get. These people could be in the form of sects that claim that they are Muslim, but are in fact outside the fold of Islaam. For example, the first of these sects to appear among Muslims were called the *Khawaarij* (the seceders). They were originally followers of the fourth Caliph, 'Alee ibn Abee Taalib, during the struggle with Mu'aawiyah they agreed to settle their differences by negotiation, a group of 'Alee's supporters broke away and declared both 'Alee and Mu'aawiyah disbelievers. This group became well known for their Qur'anic recitation and dedication to *Salaah*, but they slaughtered many Muslims who did not agree with their views. The Prophet (ﷺ) has referred to that in another *Hadeeth* in which he stated that there would be 73 sects of people all claiming to be Muslims, but only one of them would be correct.[103]

This means that merely saying that one is a Muslim or doing some of the thing that Muslims do does not guarantee that one is truly a Muslim. One's actions can cancel the value of one's faith. For example, Prophet Muhammad (ﷺ) stated that those who call to nationalism, tribalism and racism are not true Muslims.[104] He also said that whoever goes to a fortuneteller and believes what he is told has disbelieved in Islaam.[105] And, he was reported to have said that whoever wears and

---

[103] Reported by Mu'aawiyah ibn Abee Sufyaan and collected by Abu Daawood (*Sunan Abu Dawud* (English Trans.), vol.3, pp.290-291, no.4580. Authenticated by al-Albaanee in *Saheeh Sunan Abee Daawood*, vol.3, p.869, no.3843.

[104] Collected by Muslim (*Sahih Muslim* (English Trans.), vol.3, pp.1029-1030, no.4555) and an-Nasaa'ee.

[105] Collected by Ahmad, Ibn Maajah and Abu Daawood (*Sunan Abu Dawud* (English Trans.), vol.3, p.1095, no.3895) and authenticated in *Saheeh Sunan Abee Daawood*, vol.2, p.739, no.3304.

amulet has become an idol-worshipper.[106]

These people could also be hypocrites, like those who recite Qur'aan simply for money or teach Islaam only for worldly benefits. On the outside they appear to be Muslim, but on the inside they have left Islaam.

This _Hadeeth_ also addresses a big problem facing Muslims today. Many do not practice any of the pillars of Islaam, or they often disobey God's commandments in the Qur'aan. However, they have learned how to recite the Arabic text of the Qur'aan without understanding its meaning. So they will quickly pronounce the Arabic words like parrots, totally ignorant of Allaah's commands, while believing that it will earn them the rewards and cancel their evil deeds. And when one of their relatives or friends die, they will gather and divide the Qur'aan up into parts. Then they all quickly mumble the parts at the same time. And when they are finished, they ask Allaah to give the reward for their act to the dead person. However, they have taken the letter of the law and ignored the spirit. it is true that the Prophet (ﷺ) said, _"Whoever reads a single letter from Allaah's book will receive a blessing. and each blessing is worth ten times its value."_[107] Abu Umaamah also quoted him as saying, _"Recite Qur'aan, for verily it will intercede for its companions (who recite it often) on the Day of Resurrection."_[108] However, he was addressing his companions (_Sahaabah_), who all _spoke_ and _understood_ Arabic. His statements were an encouragement to read the Qur'aan often in order to absorb as much of God's commandments as possible. The more they read the Qur'aan, the more they knew what Allaah wanted of them. Their recitation of the Qur'aan had an affect on their lives. It made them better people and helped them to avoid sin. Today, in most Muslim communities, Qur'anic recitation has become a ritual used to start conferences and other social events, for competition and prestige. The meaning of God's final revelation to man has become forgotten in

---

[106] Collected by at-Tirmithee and Ahmad and authenticated in _Saheeh al-Jaami' as-Sagheer_, vol. 5, p.323, no.6270.

[107] Reported by Ibn Mas'ood and collected by at-Tirmithee (_Mishkat al-Maṣabih_ (English Trans.), vol.1,p.452) and authenticated by al-Albaanee in _Saheeh Sunan at-Tirmithee_, vol.3, p.9, no. 2327.

[108] Collected by Muslim (_Sahih Muslim_ (English Trans.), vol.2, p.385, no.1757).

many instances and the Qur'aan has become a magical charm or means of entertainment. For the recitation of the Qur'aan to go past our throats and to reach our hearts and minds, we must understand it. We have to learn the Arabic alphabet and to recite it as a step to learning the grammar and vocabulary, in order to understand its meaning. Until we master the language, we should also read the translation of the meanings in our local languages.

Lessons

1. Not all those who do the deeds of Muslims are really Muslims.
2. It is compulsory that Islaam should be practiced externally as well as internally.
3. The practices of Islaam should not become mere rituals but should be based on a firm belief in Allaah.
4. The Qur'aan should be read with understanding and not just parrotted.
5. we should beware of pretence in our various forms of worship.
6. we should reflect on the meanings of the Qur'aan and try to apply them in our lives.
7. There will appear among Muslims many sects, but the only those people who follow the *Sunnah* of the Prophet (ﷺ) are following the correct path.

QUESTIONS

1. Ibn 'Abbaas' full name was
   (a) Muhammad ibn 'Abbaas.
   (b) Ibn 'Abbaas 'Abdullaah.
   (c) 'Abdullaah ibn Muhammad ibn 'Abbaas.
   (d) 'Abdullaah ibn 'Abbaas.
   (e) 'Umar ibn 'Abbaas.

2. Ibn 'Abbaas was the Prophet's
   (a) cousin.
   (b) nephew.
   (c) uncle.
   (d) son-in-law
   (e) brother.

3. Ibn 'Abbaas was most noted as
   (a) the companion of the Prophet (ﷺ) who reported the largest number of *Hadeeths*.
   (b) the best memorizer of the Qur'aan.
   (c) the best explainer of the Qur'aan's meaning among the *Sahaabah*.
   (d) the compiler of the *Hadeeth* collection called *al-Musnad*.
   (e) the husband of the Prophet's daughter Faatimah.

4. Imaam Ahmad's full name is
   (a) Ahmad ibn 'Abbaas.
   (b) Ahmad ibn al-Musnad.
   (c) Hambal ibn Ahmad.
   (d) Imaam Ahmad ibn 'Abdullaah.
   (e) Ahmad ibn Hanbal.

5. His collection of *Hadeeths* was called
   (a) *al-Jaami' al-Musnad*.
   (b) *al-Musnad as-Saheeh*.
   (c) *al-Musnad*.
   (d) *al-Jaami*.
   (e) *Saheeh Ahmad*.

6. Imaam A<u>h</u>mad was most famous for
    (a) making the most authentic collection of <u>Hadeeths</u>.
    (b) founding the first school of Islamic law, called the <u>H</u>anafee <u>Math</u>-hab.
    (c) building a famous school in Saudi Arabia.
    (d) founding the <u>H</u>ambalee school of Islamic law.
    (e) his commentary on the Qur'aan, called al-Musnad.

7. The <u>H</u>adeeth "*There will surely be a people from my Ummah who will recite the Qur'aan, but they will fly out of Islaam like an arrow through its target*" encourage us to
    (a) learn archery
    (b) practice the rites of Islaam regularly.
    (c) only practice Islaam externally.
    (d) reflect on the meanings of the Qur'aan and not apply them.
    (e) practice Islaam internally and externally.

8. The Khawaarij were
    (a) the followers of Mu'aawiyah.
    (b) the members of 'Alee ibn Abee Taalib's family.
    (c) the first sect to recite the Qur'aan.
    (d) followers of Imaam A<u>h</u>mad's school of Islamic law.
    (e) the first sect to break away from the Muslim nation.

9. Those people who recite or teach the Qur'aan only if they are given money
    (a) are the *Khawaarij*.
    (b) are sincere believers.
    (c) only pretend to be Muslims.
    (d) are true Muslim educators.
    (e) are the followers of Mu'aawiyah.

10. Reciting the Qur'aan without understanding its meanings is
    (a) okay if one is trying to learn Arabic to understand the Qur'aan.
    (b) Strictly forbidden.
    (c) an act of disbelief.
    (d) okay because many generations or Muslims have been doing it.
    (e) okay in order to get the reward of ten blessings for each letter.

13. HADEETH FIVE: BRIBERY

عَنْ عَبْدِ اللَّهِ بْنِ عَمْرٍو قَالَ:

((لَعَنَ رَسُولُ اللَّهِ صَلَّى اللَّهُ عَلَيْهِ وَسَلَّمَ الرَّاشِيَ
وَالْمُرْتَشِيَ))

'Abdullaah ibn 'Amr said, "The Messenger of Allaah (ﷺ) cursed the one who bribes and the one who receives bribes."

Collected by at-Tirmithee[109] and Ibn Maajah

The Narrator

'Abdullaah was the son of the famous companion 'Amr ibn al-'Aas. He accepted Islaam before his father did. Before Islaam, his given name was al-'Anaas (the disobedient), and the Prophet (ﷺ) changed it to 'Abdullaah. He narrated over 700 traditions of Prophet Muhammad (ﷺ) and was among those who were given permission by the Prophet (ﷺ) to record in writing the *Hadeeths*. He was among the leading scholars of Islamic law among the *Sahaabah*. He died in Makkah around 65 A.H. (688 C.E.).[110]

The Collectors

The biography of at-Tirmithee is in *Hadeeth* number one, and that of Ibn Maajah in *Hadeeth* number four.

GENERAL MEANING

The Prophet (ﷺ) gives us a severe warning about bribery in this *Hadeeth*. He informed us that whoever gives some of his wealth to an

---

[109] *Al-Hadis* (Arabic-English), vol.1, p.523, no.300. Authenticated by al-Albaanee in *Saheeh Sunan at-Tirmithee*, vol.2, p.36, no.1074. The narration from Thawbaan, "*Allaah curses the one who bribes, the one who receives bribes and the one who arranges it,*" collected by Ahmad is not authentic (*Da'eef*). See *Da'eef al-Jaami' as-Sagheer*, vol.5, p.15, no.4687.

[110] *Siyar A'laam an-Nabalaa'*, vol.3, pp. 79-94, no.17.

authority like a judge, president or other government official, seeking to gain for himself a right which was not due to him, is cursed by Allaah because of the corruption that it will cause in society. The right he gain which was not due to him will cause someone else to be deprived of their right. The Prophet's curse is also on the person in authority who accepts the bribe in order to give someone else's right to the briber because of the corruption which is bound to result. The judge who accepts bribes cannot and will not judge justly. He will always judge in favor of those who offer him wealth, and the poor will be deprived of their legitimate rights.

The one who arranges the bribe is also included in the sin because of his taking part in oppression and corruption. He is helping the people to take the rights of others when he should be stopping them from doing so. To arrange the sale of drugs or to supply the plans for a bank robbery is to share in the sins of taking drugs and theft. Allaah commands us in the Qur'aan:

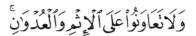

"....do not cooperate in sin and hostility."

Soorah al-Maa'idah (5) : 2

The Prophet (ﷺ) teaches us in this _Hadeeth_ to be patient, even if the only way we can obtain something is to bribe, because of the harm which will result if this method becomes widespread. The Islamic society is based on justice which can only be maintained if bribery is prohibited. The fact that many Muslim countries are today plagued with bribery, graft, kick-backs, etc., at all levels of society is evidence that they are far away from the teachings of Islaam.

Calling a bribe a "present" does not change its status. The present can be distinguished from the bribe by the fact that if the man was not in his official position, he would still receive the gift. Abu _H_umayd as-Saa'idee said, "_Allaah's Messenger appointed a man called Ibn al-Lutaybeeyah to collect_ **Zakaah** _from the Sulaym clan. When he returned, the Prophet_ (ﷺ) _called him to give account. He said to the Prophet_ (ﷺ) _'This money is for you, and this money has been given to me as a_ *gift.' The Messenger of Allaah (ﷺ) said, 'Why didn't you stay in the house of your father and mother to see whether you would receive your gift, if you are telling the truth.'"*[111] Consequently, people in official positions should not accepts gifts as long as the possibility exists that it may be seen as a bribe. Prior to or during the school year, teachers should not accept presents from their students. However, if a teacher resigns and is leaving, he or she may accept gifts of appreciation from the students.

Lesssons

1. The giving of bribes, their acceptance and their arrangement have been forbidden.
2. Whoever takes part in an act of bribery is cursed by Allaah. In this *Hadeeth*, the Prophet (ﷺ) encourages us to develop the qualities of patience and love for justice.
3. The believer must be patient to obtain his rights and must avoid the oppression of others.
4. Justice is an essential part of the Islamic society.

---

[111] Collected by al-Bukhaaree (*Sahih al-Bukhari* (Arabic-English), vol.9, pp.88-89, no.108).

QUESTIONS

1. 'Abdullaah ibn 'Amr was
    (a) the son of al-'Anas.
    (b) the father of 'Amr ibn al-'Aas.
    (c) given the name of al-'Aas by Prophet Muḥammad (ﷺ).
    (d) the son of 'Amr ibn al-'Aas.
    (e) the Prophet's uncle

2. He was most noted as
    (a) a commentator on the Qur'aan.
    (b) the companion who narrated the most traditions of the Prophet (ﷺ).
    (c) one of the leading scholars of Islamic law among the companions.
    (d) the collector of the *Hadeeth* on bribery.
    (e) the son of one of the Prophet's companions.

3. The Prophet (ﷺ) changed 'Abdullaah's name
    (a) from al-'Aas to 'Amr.
    (b) because he adopted him.
    (c) from 'Abdullaah to al-'Aas.
    (d) because his previous name had a bad meaning.
    (e) to 'Abdullaah from 'Amr.

4. If bribery is allowed in society, it
    (a) makes business dealing run more smoothly and faster.
    (b) favours the rich over the poor.
    (c) would help judges to make their rulings more easily.
    (d) would make the poor strong and oppress the richer classes.
    (e) will give the society a firm basis for justice and equality.

5. Bribery is a form of oppression because it
    (a) gives people their rights.
    (b) denies people what does not belong to them.
    (c) prohibits the rich from taking the rights of the poor.
    (d) gives some people the rights of others.
    (e) takes wealth away from the rich and gives it to the poor.

6. The one who arranges the bribe is also involved in sin because
   (a) the Prophet (ﷺ) said so.
   (b) because he benefits in the same way that the one who received the bribe does.
   (c) he is helping others commit a sin.
   (d) thinking about a sin is the same as committing it.
   (e) the definition of bribery includes the witness.

7. In this _Hadeeth_, the Prophet (ﷺ) is in fact encouraging us to
   (a) avoid taking bribes, but we may receive them.
   (b) give bribes, but not demand them.
   (c) neither give or take bribes, but we may arrange them for others.
   (d) avoid bribery completely.
   (e) curse those who give or take bribes

14. HADEETH SIX:
CONSIDERING THE FEELINGS OF OTHERS

عَنْ عَبْدِاللَّهِ رَضِيَ اللَّهُ عَنْهُ أَنَّ رَسُـولَ اللَّهِ صَلَّى اللَّهُ عَلَيْهِ وَسَلَّمَ
قَالَ :

((إِذَا كَانُوا ثَلاَثَةً فَلاَ يَتَنَاجَى اثْنَانِ دُونَ الثَّالِثِ))

Naafi' reported from Ibn 'Umar that Allaah's Messenger (ﷺ) said, "If there are three (persons), two of them should not talk privately to the exclusion of the third."

It is agreed upon.[112]

The Narrator

Naafi' was the *Mawlaa*[113] of the great companion 'Abdullaah ibn 'Umar. He was originally from Persia and later became one of the foremost scholars and narrators of *Hadeeth* among the *Taabe'oon*. In fact, Imaam Bukhaaree said that the best chain of narration was that of Naafi' from Ibn 'Umar. Later, Caliph 'Umar ibn 'Abdul 'Azeez put Naafi' in charge of collecting *Zakaah*. Naafi' died in the year 118 A.H. (736 C.E.).[114]

The Collectors

The biographies of al-Bukhaaree and Muslim can be found in *Hadeeth* number three and Abu Daawood's in number one.

GENERAL MEANING

The Prophet (ﷺ) informs us in this *Hadeeth* of a principle which is critical for the smooth running of the society. This principle is concern

---

[112] "Agreed upon" means that the *Hadeeth* was collected by the two most famous collectors of *Hadeeth*, al-Bukhaaree and Muslim. Collected by al-Bukhaaree (*Sahih al-Bukhari* (Arabic-English), vol.8, p. 203, no.303), Muslim (*Sahih Muslim* (English Trans.), vol.3, p.1191, no.5419) and Abu Daawood (*Sunan Abu Dawud* (English Trans.), vol.3, p.1354, no.4833).

[113] The freed slave of a person.

[114] *Siyar A'laam an-Nubalaa'*, vol.5, pp. 95-101, no. 34.

and consideration for the feelings of others. We are instructed to avoid private conversations in the company of others because this leads to doubt and suspicion. When one sees or hears others talking privately or secretly in his presence, he immediately wonders what they are trying to hide from him.

The thought usually comes to one who is excluded from the conversation that he is being talked about. Because Islaam opposes all things which could cause suspicion and bad feelings, it demands that we speak openly if we are in the company of others.

If there are four people, and two talk privately, it is permitted because the other two can communicate between themselves and the likelihood of suspicion is small since it is not just one person being excluded. However, if three of the four talk privately excluding one, the same conditions are present. Consequently, whenever only one is excluded from the conversation, the prohibition applies.

This _Hadeeth_ also refers to speaking in a language unfamiliar to others in order to convey things privately. This habit should also be avoided, as it creates the same suspicious and a common language of communication should be used whenever possible.

The prohibition in this _Hadeeth_ is part of a general prohibition in Islaam against secrecy. Almighty Allaah said,

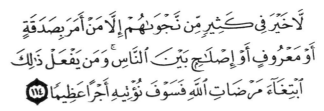

There is no good in most of their secret talks except (in the talks of) he who enjoins charity, righteous deeds, or conciliation among people. And he who does this seeking the pleasure of Allaah, we will give a great reward."

Soorah an-Nisaa' (4) : 114

Secret societies like the Masons, Rosicrucians, etc. provide good for their members at the expense of the general public. Thus, they are generally evil. Their members plot and plan ways to exploit the society. When they do charitable works, it is only a cover for their secret activities.

Lessons

1. Speaking privately in the company of others is forbidden if one person is excluded.
2. Islaam is very concerned about the removal of things or habits which may hurt the feelings of others.
3. Islaam is also concerned with the removal of things which cause doubts or suspicions.
4. In this *Hadeeth*, the Prophet (ﷺ) encourages the development of sympathy and trust among Muslims.

QUESTIONS

1. Naafi' was the
   (a) son of Ibn 'Umar.
   (b) father of Ibn 'Umar.
   (c) freed slave of Ibn 'Umar.
   (d) slave of 'Umar.
   (e) son of *Mawlaa*.

2. The chain of narration from Ibn 'Umar through Naafi' was
   (a) considered the longest by al-Bukhaaree.
   (b) agreed upon by Muslim scholars.
   (c) reported only by Muslims.
   (d) classified as the best by al-Bukhaaree.
   (e) collected only by Imaam al-Bukhaaree in his book of *Hadeeths*.

3. "Agreed upon" in reference to *Hadeeth* means that
   (a) the *Hadeeth* was reported by the two most famous companions.
   (b) it was reported by all of the famous collectors of *Hadeeth*.
   (c) the Prophet (ﷺ) approved of the *Hadeeth*.
   (d) it could be found in both *Saheeh al-Bukhaaree* and *Saheeh Muslim*.
   (e) the *Hadeeth* was collected by the two famous collectors of *Hadeeth*, al-Bukhaaree and Abu Daawood.

4. We shouldn't speak privately in the company of others because
   (a) they will think that we are talking about them, causing suspicion and hurt feelings.
   (b) it is preferred to talk about people when they are not in our presence.
   (c) secret talks are absolutely forbidden in Islaam.
   (d) it is preferable to speak in a different language when we don't want others to know what we are saying.
   (e) they may hear only part of what we are saying and misunderstand.

5. If there are five people talking, and four of them talk privately excluding the fifth, it is

> (a) permissible because the _Hadeeth_ only applies to groups of three.
>
> (b) permissible if they talk in another language unknown to the fifth person.
>
> (c) prohibited only if they speak in another language.
>
> (d) prohibited because the forbidden principle of excluding a single person from conversation also exists in this case.
>
> (e) not considered prohibited if only one person is excluded.

15. HADEETH SEVEN: BACKBITING

عَنْ أَبِي هُرَيْرَةَ أَنَّ رَسُولَ اللّهِ صَلَّى اللّهُ عَلَيْهِ وَسَلَّمَ قَالَ :

((أَتَدْرُونَ مَا الْغِيبَةُ ؟)) قَالُوا اللّهُ وَرَسُولُهُ أَعْلَمُ قَالَ:((ذِكْرُكَ

أَخَاكَ بِمَا يَكْرَهُ)) قِيلَ أَفَرَأَيْتَ إِنْ كَانَ فِي أَخِي مَا أَقُولُ

قَالَ:((إِنْ كَانَ فِيهِ مَا تَقُولُ فَقَدِ اغْتَبْتَهُ وَإِنْ لَمْ يَكُنْ فِيهِ فَقَدْ

بَهَتَّهُ))

Abu Hurayrah reported that Allaah's Messenger (ﷺ) said, "Do you know what backbiting is?" The Companions replied, "Allaah and His Prophet alone know." He said, "It is mentioning about your brother what he dislikes." One of the Companions asked, "What if what I say about him is true?" He replied, " If what you say about him is true, you have backbitten, and if it isn't true you have slandered him."

Collected by Muslim and Abu Daawood[115]

The Narrator

Abu Hurayrah's biography can be found in *Hadeeth* number two.

The Collectors

The biography of Muslim can be found in *Hadeeth* number three and Abu Daawood's in *Hadeeth* number one.

GENERAL MEANING

This *Hadeeth* is a kind of *Tafseer* of Allaah's command in Soorah al-Hujuraat, "**Don't backbite each other**" (49:10). The Prophet (ﷺ) also cleared up a widespread and dangerous misconception concerning back-

---

[115] *Sahih Muslim* (English Trans.), vol.4, p. 1369, no.6265; *Sunan Abu Dawud* (English Trans.), vol.3, pp. 1358-1359, no.4856.

biting, which is that it is only telling lies about someone behind his back. First of all, the Prophet (ﷺ) defined backbiting in general terms, saying that it was that which one would not like said about himself. When one of the Companions raised the misconception that if what we said was true, it would be all right, the Prophet (ﷺ) gave a specific definition of backbiting. Backbiting is the mention of someone's faults behind his back, and the mention of fabricated faults is slander.

Backbiting is _Haraam_ because it is an attack on a Muslim's honor. It exposes weaknesses which need not be exposed. It lowers him in the eyes of others, thereby causing others to scorn him and act contemptuously towards him. This destroys the things which bind a Muslim society. The Prophet (ﷺ) not only forbade backbiting, but also attacked many of the paths leading to it. For example, he forbade suspicion saying, "*Beware of suspicion, for verily it is the most deceptive from of conversation.*"[116] The reason for this is that suspicion often leads people to talk about others.

Allaah also forbade jealousy saying, "*Do not hate each other, and do not be jealous of each other...*"[117] Jealousy often leads people to speak badly about others in an attempt to ruin the successes which they have been blessed with. In that way, jealousy can easily lead to the even greater crimes of backbiting and slander.

The Prophet (ﷺ) provided a practical alternative to talking about others' faults by advising us to see in others our own faults. He said, "*The believer is a mirror image of his brother.*"[118] If one becomes involved in correcting his own faults and strengthening his own weaknesses, he really would not have time to indulge in idle conversations about others. Whenever he sees imperfections in the character of others, it would only remind him of his own imperfections.

---

[116] Reported by Abu Hurayrah and Collected by al-Bukhaaree (_Sahih al-Bukhari_ (Arabic-English), vol.8, p.58, no.90), Muslim (_Sahih Muslim_ (English Trans.), vol.4, p.1361, no.6214) and Abu Daawood (_Sunan Abu Dawud_ (English Trans.), vol.3, p.1370, no.4899).

[117] Collected by al-Bukhaaree (_Sahih al-Bukhari_ (Arabic-English), vol.8, p.58, no.91).

[118] Reported by Abu Hurayrah and collected by Abu Daawood, authenticated by al-Albaanee in _Saheeh Sunan Abee Daawood_, vol. 3, p.929, no.4110.

The Prophet (ﷺ) placed another subtle barrier in the way of backbiting by pointing out the reward for those who defend the honor of their brother Muslims. Abu ad-Dardaa' reported that the Prophet (ﷺ) said, *"On the Day of Resurrection, Allaah will deflect the fire from they face of whoever defends his Muslim brother's honor in the latter's absence."*

The *Sharee'ah* in Islaam has placed a stiff penalty on those who slander the chastity of believing women. Allaah said in the Qur'aan,

$$وَٱلَّذِينَ يَرۡمُونَ ٱلۡمُحۡصَنَٰتِ ثُمَّ لَمۡ يَأۡتُواْ بِأَرۡبَعَةِ شُهَدَآءَ فَٱجۡلِدُوهُمۡ ثَمَٰنِينَ جَلۡدَةٗ$$

**"Those who accuse chaste women and fail to produce
four witnesses should be lashed eighty times.**

Soorah an-Noor (24) : 4

When this verse was revealed, the Prophet (ﷺ) ordered that two of the *Sahaabah*, Hassan ibn Thaabit and Mistah ibn Uthaathah, and a *Sahaabeeyah*,[119] Hamnah bint Jahsh, be lashed for slandering 'Aa'eshah.[120]

For slander of a lower level, the judge in an Islamic state is allowed to set an appropriate punishment, which may be jail, a fine, lashing or another punishment, according to the seriousness of the case and the position of the parties involved.

In any case, slander is considered a serious and punishable crime even in western nations due to the fact that if it were left uncontrolled, it would tear at the very fabric of the society. Bonds of marriage, family and friendship would come apart and suspicion would dominate all social relationships, eventually leading to a crumbling of all the institutions within the society. The final result would be total anarchy and chaos as the law of the jungle, survival of the fittest, gains way.

Therefore, Islaam has placed numerous barriers in the way of lying, suspicion, backbiting and slander in order to protect the members of

---

[119] female companion of the Prophet (ﷺ).

[120] Reported by 'Aa'eshah and collected by the writers of the *Sunans*.

the Islamic society from the devastating effects of these and other vices. This clearly shows that Islaam in not simply a religion which deals only with spiritual affairs, but it is a way of life that covers both the spiritual and material needs of mankind and is suitable for application in all times.

Lessons

1. Backbiting is forbidden in Islaam because it attacks the honor of Muslims.
2. The Prophet (ﷺ) forbade things which could lead to backbiting, such as suspicion and jealousy.
3. A Muslim should spend his time correcting his own faults instead of looking for faults in others.
4. Muslims should protect the honor of Muslims.
5. Slander is a very serious offense in Islaam and is punishable under the *Sharee'ah*.
6. Islaam is a practical religion that seeks to protect the individual and the society from harmful vices.

QUESTIONS

1. Abu Hurayrah was
   (a) given his name by Prophet Muḥammad (ﷺ)
   (b) originally from Persia.
   (c) called 'Abdur-Raḥmaan ibn Sakhr before accepting Islaam.
   (d) one of the greatest legal scholars among the *Sahaabah*.
   (e) noted as having made the most authentic collection on *Hadeeths*.

2. Muslim was
   (a) an early convert to Islaam.
   (b) noted for having the second most authentic collection of *Hadeeths*.
   (c) known for having narrated the largest number of *Hadeeths* of any of the *Sahaabah*.
   (d) originally named Muhammad ibn Ismaa'eel.
   (e) born in Madeenah.

3. Backbiting is
   (a) saying something about a person which is not true.
   (b) mentioning something about a person whom you do not like.
   (c) mentioning the good points of others.
   (d) saying anything about a person which they would not like you to say.
   (e) saying something about a person that they would not mind you saying.

4. Backbiting is forbidden in Islaam because
   (a) it attacks the honor of Muslims and destroys the bonds of brotherhood.
   (b) speaking about a person in their absence is cowardly and Islaam encourages bravery.
   (c) it involves lying, which is *Haraam* according to the teaching of Islaam.
   (d) it is based on jealousy, from which Allaah advises us to seek refuge in *Soorah al-Falaq*.
   (e) none of the above.

5. Explain how suspicion and jealousy can lead to backbiting.

6. The Prophet (ﷺ) encouraged us to avoid backbiting by
(a) commanding us to tell the truth about others, even behind their backs.
(b) requiring us to seek Allaah's forgiveness whenever we slander others.
(c) advising us to see the faults of others in ourselves.
(d) prohibiting us from speaking the truth about others.
(e) promising eternal damnation in hell for those who backbite

7. Islaam deals severely with those who slander chaste women
(a) because women are inferior to men.
(b) in order to liberate women from the oppression of men.
(c) in the same way that it does with those who slander innocent men.
(d) because the honour or women is more important than the honour of men.
(e) because a slandered woman will have great difficulty in getter married later.

16. USOOL AL-FIQH: LEGAL CATEGORIES

All things are divided into two main categories: those which are permissible, known as *Halaal*, and those which are forbidden, known as *Haraam*. There is nothing in existence which does not fall under one of these categories.

HALAAL (PERMISSIBLE)

The category of *Halaal* is further divided into four sub-Divisions based on the way in which they were made allowable:

1. Waajib of Fard (Obligatory)

The act which is considered *Waajib* must be done. If one does it he is rewarded by Allaah, and if he fails to do it (purposely) he has committed a sin and will be punished. How do we know if something is *Waajib*? If Allaah or His Prophet (ﷺ) has ordered us to do something without making any exceptions, it is considered *Waajib*. The proof of this is in Allaah's statement in the Qur'aan.

وَمَآءَاتَنكُمُ ٱلرَّسُولُ فَخُذُوهُ وَمَا نَهَنكُمْ عَنْهُ فَٱنتَهُواْ

> "Whatever the Prophet orders you, do it, and whatever he forbids you, leave it!"
>
> Soorah al-Hashr (59) : 7

The Qur'aan orders us to worship Allaah without partners, establish regular *Salaah* and pay our *Zakaah* in *Soorah* al-Bayyinah (97), verse 5:

وَمَآ أُمِرُوٓاْ إِلَّا لِيَعۡبُدُواْ ٱللَّهَ مُخۡلِصِينَ لَهُ ٱلدِّينَ حُنَفَآءَ
وَيُقِيمُواْ ٱلصَّلَوٰةَ وَيُؤۡتُواْ ٱلزَّكَوٰةَ ۚ وَذَٰلِكَ دِينُ ٱلۡقَيِّمَةِ ۝

> "And they were only ordered to worship Allaah, alone, establish their *Salaah* and pay their *Zakaah*. That is the real religion."

Therefore, it is *Waajib* that we worship only Allaah, pray our five daily *Salaah* and give our yearly *Zakaah* to the poor. If we do we will be greatly rewarded by Allaah, but if we worship someone or something other than Allaah, leave our *Salaah* or refuse to pay our *Zakaah*, we will be punished.

The Prophet (☀) commanded us saying, *"Pray all of you just as you saw me pray."*[121] Therefore, it is *Waajib* on all Muslims to pray in some way that the last Prophet (☀) prayed. If we do so, we will get the full reward of *Salaah*, but if we know the right way and pray another way, we will be punished by Allaah and our *Salaah* will not be accepted.

2. Mustahabb (Recommended)

The act which is *Mustahabb* is one which the Prophet (☀) has encouraged us to do. If someone does it, he will be rewarded by Allaah, but if he doesn't do it, he has not done a sin and will not be punished. The *Mustahabb* things are there to help us get used to obeying Allaah and His Prophet (☀) so that when we are given something *Waajib* to do, it will be easier for us to do it. It is also a means by which one can make up for the mistakes made in *Fard* acts.

How do we know when something is *Mustahabb*? Acts classified as *Mustahabb* are those which (a) the Prophet (☀) used to do regularly, (b) those he recommended that we do, (c) those which he ordered to be done and then later allowed not to be done, or (d) those which he prohibited and then later commanded. All such acts are *Mustahabb*. For example, the Prophet (☀) used to pray two *Raka'aat*[122] of voluntary prayer before doing the *Fard Salaah* of *Fajr*, even when he was travelling and stopped doing other prayers before and after the other compulsory prayers.[123] Thus, it is considered *Mustahabb* for us to pray these

---

[121] Collected by al-Bukhaaree (*Sahih al-Bukhari* (Arabic-English), vol.1, p.345, no.604).

[122] Units of prayer.

[123] Collected by al-Bukhaaree (*Sahih* al-Bukhari (Arabic-English), vol.2, p.144, no.260), Muslim (*Sahih* Muslim (English Trans.), vol.1,p.351, no.1568) and Abu Daawood (*Sunan Abu Dawud* (English Trans.), vol.1, p.329, no.1249).

two *Raka'aat* whenever possible. The Prophet (ﷺ) also encouraged us to fast on certain days in the year outside the month of *Ramadaan*. For example, he said that if we fasted six days in the month of *Shawwaal*[124] along with the whole month of *Ramadaan*, we would get the reward for fasting the whole year.[125] Similarly, he also recommended *'Umrah* in *Ramadaan* by saying that one who does so is as one who made *Hajj* with him.[126] An example of the third type of Mustahabb act is the command for Ghusl (Islamic bath) on Friday. Initially the Prophet (ﷺ) said that *"Ghusl on Friday is compulsory on everyone reaching puberty."*[127] but he later said, *"Whoever makes **Wudoo'** on Friday is blessed, but making the **Ghusl** is better."*[128] And an example of the fourth kind in which a previously prohibited act was later ordered is the command to visit graves. Regarding this, the Prophet (ﷺ) said, *"I used to prohibit you from visiting the graves, (but now) visit them, as it will remind (of the next life)."*[129]

3.   Mubaah (Allowed)

The act which is considered *Mubaah* is one which hasn't been ordered, recommended, disliked or forbidden by Allaah and His Prophet (ﷺ).[130] It is something optional, meaning that we may or may not do it. If we do it without any particular intention, there is no reward from Allaah, and if we do not, there is no punishment. The category of *Mubaah* increases the area of *Halaal* acts and gives man more freedom of choice so that he has no reason for going to the *Haraam*. Examples of things

---

[124] The 10th month of the lunar calendar, which is the month immediately following *Ramadaan*.

[125]   Collected by Muslim (*Sahih Muslim* (English Trans.), vol.2, p.570, no.2614) and Abu Daawood (*Sunan Abu Dawud* (English Trans.), vol.2, p.669, no.2427

[126]   Collected by Abu Daawood (*Sunan Abu Dawud* (English Trans.), vol.2, p.527, no.1985).

[127]   Collected by al-Bukhaaree (*Sahih al-Bukhari* (Arabic-English), vol.2, p.9, no.20).

[128]   Collected by Abu Daawood (*Sunan Abu Dawud* (English Trans.), vol.1, p.93, no.356) and authenticated (*Hasan*) in *Saheeh Sunan Abee Daawood*, vol.1, p.72, no.341.

[129] Collected by Abu Daawood (*Sunan Abu Dawud* (English Trans.), vol.2, p.919, no.3229) from Buraydah, and authenticated by al-Albaanee in *Saheeh al-Jaami' as-Sagheer*, vol.4, p.187, no.4460 from Anas in *al-Mustadrak*.

[130]   i.e. by Allaah and His Prophet.

that are *Mubaah* are taking a bath on a hot day to cool off, buying a Pepsi instead of a Mirinda, or scratching your head with your left hand or right hand.

Khaalid ibn al-Waleed related that he went with Allaah's Messenger (ﷺ) to visit Khaalid's aunt Maymoonah, who was one of the Prophet's wives, and found that she had roasted a Dabb (a large desert lizard). When she offered the lizard (dish) to Allaah's Messenger (ﷺ), he refused it, so Khaalid asked him if lizards were prohibited. He replied, "No, but there were none in my people's land and I find that I dislike them." Khaalid said, "I then bit off a piece, chewed and ate it with the Prophet (ﷺ) looking at me."[131] Eating *Dabb* is therefore *Mubaah*. The Prophet (ﷺ) disliked it personally, but permitted it for others.

4. Makrooh (Disliked)

The act which is considered *Makrooh* is the one which Allaah or His Prophet (ﷺ) has described as being nasty or disgusting or one which the Prophet (ﷺ) forbade but later did to let us know that it is not a sin and that it was only disliked. This category of actions contains some form of harm in them. The harm may be physical of spiritual, however, the effects are not serious enough to have the acts prohibited. For example, the father of Ya'eesh ibn Tikhafah said, *"While I was lying on my stomach in the early morning, a man began to nudge me with his foot and then said, "This is a method of lying which God hates." When I looked up I saw that it was Allaah's Messenger."*[132] After extensive research into spinal ailments and their causes, specialists from the medical profession made the following recommendations: "Poor sleep posture is a sure invitation to backaches. Use a firm mattress. Lie on the side with a bend to the knees. Avoid lying on the belly, a position that increases the lumber curve, causing that familiar sagging called swayback."[133] Thus, the avoidance of sleeping on the stomach does protect

---

[131] Collected by al-Bukhaaree (*Sahih al-Bukhari* (Arabic English), vol.7, pp. 230-231, no.303) and Muslim (*Sahih Muslim* (English Trans.), vol.3, p.1074, no.4790).

[132] Collected by Abu Daawood (*Sunan Abu Dawud* (English Trans.), vol.3, pp.1400-1401, no.502) and Ibn Maajah, and authenticated in *Saheeh Sunan Ibn Maajah*, vol.2, p.305, no.3000.

[133] Time Magazine (European Edition: July 4, 1980), p.34.

man from some physical harm. There may also be other physical harm as well as spiritual harm unknown to us.

We are encouraged to avoid the *Makrooh* acts since they are close to being forbidden. Avoiding *Makrooh* acts trains man in self-control to make the avoidance of *Haraam* acts easier. If we avoid them, we will be rewarded by Allaah, but if we do them, there is no punishment. If someone gets into the habit of doing *Makrooh* things it will be easy for him to fall into the forbidden things. So, we should avoid them as much as possible.

For example, the Prophet (🕮) said, *"The one who plays backgammon is like one who dyes his hand in the blood of swine."*[134] Since dyeing one's hand in pig's blood is a nasty act, so is playing backgammon, so we should avoid it and games that are similar to it. If we do so, Allaah will reward us, but if we insist on playing it, we will likely end up playing it for money and fall into the sin of gambling, which is strictly forbidden and punishable in this life and the next.

An example of the second category can be found in the Prophet's pro-hibition of drinking while standing. Abu Hurayrah quoted Allaah's Messenger (🕮) as saying, *"None of you should drink while standing; And if anyone forgets, he should vomit."*[135] However, the Prophet (🕮) was also known to have drank while standing. 'Alee ibn Abee Taalib prayed the noon prayer and then sat down in the wide courtyard (of the Masjid) of Kufah in order to deal with the affairs of the people until '*Asr* prayer. Water was then brought to him. He drank some of it, made *Wudoo'*, then stood up and drank the remaining water while standing and said, *"Some people dislike to drink water while standing, but the Prophet (🕮) did as I have just done."*[136]

---

[134] Collected by Muslim (*Sahih Muslim* (English Trans.) vol.4, p.1222, no.5612) and Abu Daawood (*Sunan Abu Dawud* (English Trans.), vol.3, p.1374, no.4920).
[135] Collected by Muslim (*Sahih Muslim* (English Trans.), vol.3, p.1117, no.5022.
[136] Collected by al-Bukhaaree (*Sahih al-Bukhari* (Arabic-English), vol.7, p.358, no.520).

HARAAM (FORBIDDEN)

An act is considered *Haraam* if Allaah or His Messenger (ﷺ) ordered us not to do it, without making any exceptions. If we avoid such an act, we will be rewarded by Allaah, but if we do it, we have sinned and will be punished.

How do we know when something is *Haraam*? An act is considered *Haraam* if Allaah or His Prophet (ﷺ) said that:

(1) It is forbidden by either using the term "forbidden" or by saying " do not." For example, the Prophet (ﷺ) said, "*Don't eat with your left hand, for surely Satan eats with his left hand.*"[137] Allaah said in the Qur'aan:

حُرِّمَتْ عَلَيْكُمْ أُمَّهَٰتُكُمْ
وَبَنَاتُكُمْ وَأَخَوَاتُكُمْ وَعَمَّاتُكُمْ وَخَالَاتُكُمْ

"Forbidden to you (in marriage) are: your mothers, your daughters, your sister, your father's sisters, your mother's sisters..."

Soorah an-Nisaa' (4) : 23

(2) We should avoid it totally as Allaah stated in the Qur'aan:

إِنَّمَا الْخَمْرُ وَالْمَيْسِرُ وَالْأَنصَابُ وَالْأَزْلَٰمُ رِجْسٌ
مِّنْ عَمَلِ الشَّيْطَٰنِ فَاجْتَنِبُوهُ لَعَلَّكُمْ تُفْلِحُونَ

"Verily alcohol gambling and fortunetelling are filth from the work of Satan, so avoid them totally in order to be successful."

Soorah al-Maa'idah (5) : 90

---

[137] Collected by Muslim (*Sahih Muslim* (English Trans.), vol.3, p.1115, no.5010) and Abu Daawood (*Sunan Abu Dawud* (English Trans.), vol.3, p.1065, no.3767).

(3) It is punishable in the *Sharee'ah*. 'Uqbah ib al-Haarith said, "*An-Nu'maan or his son was brought to the Prophet (ﷺ) in state of drunkenness. The Prophet (ﷺ) took it hard and ordered those present in the house to give him a beating. They all took part in flogging him with the stalks of the date palm and shoes, and I was among those who beat him.*"[138]

(4) Whoever does it will burn in Hellfire. Haarithah ibn Wahb reported that Allaah's Messenger (ﷺ) said, "*.... Shall I inform you of the people of Hell?*" *And the companions replied,* "*Yes.*" *The Prophet (ﷺ) then said,* "*Every haughty, fat (from overeating) and proud person.*"[139] Or that they will not enter Paradise, as in the Prophet's statement, "*The gossiper will not enter Paradise.*"[140]

(5) It is cursed. For example, Abu Hurayrah said, "*Allaah's Messenger (ﷺ) cursed men who dressed like women and women who dressed like men.*"[141] Ibn Abee Mulaykah also reported that when someone asked 'Aa'ishah if a women could wear men's sandals, she replied, "*Allaah's Messenger (ﷺ) cursed mannish women.*"

The purpose behind the category of *Haraam* acts is:

(i) to protect man from things which are extremely harmful to himself and society, either physically (like alcohol) or spiritually (like pride).
(ii) to test man's faith and differentiate between true believers, weak believers and disbelievers.
(iii) to help develop man's awareness of Allaah by forcing him to refrain from certain acts even though he may not be able to perceive the harm in it.

---

[138] Collected by al-Bukhaaree (*Sahih al-Bukhari* (Arabic -English), vol.8, p.505, no.766).

[139] Collected by Muslim (*Sahih Muslim* (English Trans.) vol.4, p.1485, no.6833).

[140] Collected by al-Bukhaaree (*Sahih al-Bukhari* (Arabic-English), vol.8, p.52, no.82).

[141] Collected by Abu Daawood (*Sunan Abu Dawud* (English Trans.), vol.3, p.1143, no.4087).

QUESTIONS

1. If someone does a *Makrooh* act, he
    (a) earns a reward for himself, as there is no sin in doing it.
    (b) earns a punishment for himself, as there is a sin in doing it.
    (c) earns no reward for himself, as there is a sin in doing it.
    (d) earns no reward for himself, as there is no sin in doing it.
    (e) earns no punishment for himself, though there is a sin in doing it.

2. An act is classified as *Mustahabb* if
    (a) the Prophet (ﷺ) did the act regularly and expressed his dislike for it.
    (b) Allaah or the Prophet (ﷺ) expressed dislike for it.
    (c) it has neither been ordered, recommended, disliked or forbidden by Allaah or His Prophet (ﷺ).
    (d) the Prophet (ﷺ) recommended it or did it regularly.
    (e) no punishment has been put in Islamic law for doing it.

3. If the Prophet (ﷺ) forbade something, then later ordered it, it is considered to be
    (a) *Waajib.*
    (b) *Mustahabb.*
    (c) *Mubaah.*
    (d) *Makrooh.*
    (e) *Haraam*

4. One who chooses not to do a *Haraam* act will be
    (a) punished, as such an act is a sin.
    (b) rewarded, as such an act is not a sin.
    (c) punished, though the act is not sinful.
    (d) rewarded, if the act is not sinful.
    (e) rewarded, since the act is sinful.

5. Not doing an act which the Prophet (ﷺ) encouraged us to do
    (a) is a sin which will earn us a punishment.
    (b) is not a sin, but will earn us a punishment.
    (c) is a sin, but will earn us a reward.

(d) is not a sin, but will earn us a reward.

(e) is not a sin and will not earn us a reward.

6. *Halaal* acts are all considered to be
    (a) *Waajib.*
    (b) *Mustahabb.*
    (c) *Mubaah.*
    (d) *Makrooh.*
    (e) none of the above.

7. The purpose behind the category of *Haraam* is
    (a) to punish man for his disobedience to Allaah.
    (b) to test man's obedience to Satan.
    (c) to take away some of the good things of this life as a test for man.
    (d) to encourage man to earn rewards for himself.
    (e) to prevent man from harming himself and society.

8. One of the purposes behind the category of *Makrooh* is
    (a) to guide man to the most beneficial acts.
    (b) that by doing *Makrooh* acts one more easily avoids the *Haraam.*
    (c) to decrease tha area of *Halaal* acts and give man more freedom to do the *Haraam.*
    (d) that by avoiding the *Makrooh*, one is trained in self-control.
    (e) to encourage man to avoid doing those things which are *Waajib.*

9. Allaah says in the Qur'aan, "**But the devils disbelieved by teaching the people magic.**"[142]
    (a) *Halaal* because it is an act of desbelief only for devils.
    (b) *Makrooh* because it is disliked by Allaah.
    (c) *Mubaah* because the Prophet (ﷺ) did not prohibit or dislike it.
    (d) *Haraam* because those doing it become disbelievers.
    (e) *Haraam* only if one teaches it as well

---

[142] Soorah al-Baqarah (2) : 102.

10. 'Alee ibn Abee Taalib said, "*Allaah's Messenger* (ﷺ) *held some silk cloth in his left hand and some gold in his right and said, 'Both of these are prohibited for the males of my community.'*" For women to wear silk is

   (a) *Waajib* because it was prohibited for males.

   (b) *Haraam* if they wear it on their left hands.

   (c) *Mubaah* because it was not prohibited, commanded, disliked or recommended.

   (d) *Makrooh* because it was prohibited for males.

   (e) *Mustahabb* because the Prophet (ﷺ) always wore it

11. Roller-skating is said to be better than ice-skating. To roller-skate is

   (a) *Mustahabb* if one does not ice-skate.

   (b) *Mubaah* if one does not ice-skate.

   (c) *Makrooh* because it was not recommended by the Prophet (ﷺ)

   (d) *Waajib* because it is compulsory for us to do better things.

   (e) *Mubaah* because it was not prohibited, commanded, disliked or recommended by Allaah or His Prophet (ﷺ).

12. Abu Hurayrah quoted Prophet Muhammad (ﷺ) as saying, "the part of the lower garment (*Izaar*) which hangs below the ankles is in the fire."[143] For men to wear pants which hang below the ankles is considered in Islamic law to be

   (a) *Halaal* because pants are not lower garments.

   (b) *Makrooh* since the Prophet (ﷺ) only disliked doing so.

   (c) *Haraam* if the pants look like a lower garment.

   (d) *Makrooh* because the Prophet (ﷺ) did not forbid it.

   (e) *Haraam* since doing so is connected with the Hellfire.

---

[143] Collected by al-Bukhaaree (*Sahih al-Bukhari* (Arabic English), vol.7, pp. 456-457, no.678).

13. Allaah said in the Qur'aan, "**Cut off the hand of the male and female thief**."[144] Stealing is classified as
>   (a) *Makrooh* since it is disliked by Alllaah.
>   (b) *Haraam* because its punishment is the Hellfire.
>   (c) *Makrooh* if one steals with his or her feet.
>   (d) *Haraam* since there is a punishment in the *Sharee'ah* for it.
>   (e) *Haraam* because one who does so becomes a disbeliever.

14. The Prophet (ﷺ) was quoted by Anas as saying, "*Seeking knowledge is obligatory for every Muslim.*" To not learn is
>   (a) *Mubaah* since it is obligatory to seek knowledge.
>   (a) *Waajib* because the Prophet (ﷺ) said it was obligatory.
>   (a) *Haraam* because not doing something *Waajib* is a sin and all sins are *Haraam*.
>   (a) *Mustahabb* if one's teachers are not nice.
>   (a) *Haraam* because the punishment is burning in Hell forever.

---

[144] Soorah al-Maa'idah (5) : 38.

153

17. FIQH: AS-SALAAH

Definition

Literally, *Salaah* means *Du'aa*, which is simply prayer without any special form or specified time. But Islamically, *Salaah* represents the prescribed actions and sayings done between the opening *Takbeer* (saying "*Allaahu akbar*") and the closing *Tasleem* (saying "*Assalaamu 'alaykum*").[145]

THE IMPORTANCE OF SALAAH IN ISLAAM

Salaah, without a doubt, is the most important form of worship which Allaah has prescribed for man. It represents the back bone of Islaam, for just as the removal of the spine would cause a man's body to crumple up in a heap, leaving him unable to stand straight, likewise the loss of *Salaah* would cause an individual's Islaam to become a meaningless jumble of rituals. Because of that, the Prophet (ﷺ) said, "*Between a man and disbelief is **Salaah**.*"[146] That is, if a man stops praying, he automatically falls into *Kufr*, even if he continues to claim that he is a Muslim and makes *Hajj*, '*Umrah*, fasts in *Ramadaan* and pays *Zakaah*. The Prophet (ﷺ) further emphasized the importance of *Salaah* in a Muslim's life by comparing it to a camel's spine and saying that "*The head of all affairs is Islaam, its spine is Salaah and the top of its hump is **Jihaad** in Allaah's path.*"[147] In fact, the very last piece of advice which the Prophet (ﷺ) left his *Ummah* was to guard their *Salaah*. On his death-bed, his last words were "*As-salaah, as-salaah.*"[148]

---

[145] Collected by Abu Daawood (*Sunan Abu Dawud* (English Trans.), vol.1 ,p. 15, no.61).

[146] Reported by Jaabir and collected by Muslim (*Sahih Muslim* (English Trans), vol.1, p.49, no.147) and Ahmad.

[147] Narrated by Mu'aath and collected by at-Tirmithee and Ibn Maajah. Authenticated by al-Albaanee is *Saheeh Sunan at-Tirmithee*, vol.2, pp.328-329, no.2110.

[148] Narrated by Anas and collected by Ahmad (Musnad Ahmad, vol.1, p.78), an -Nasaa'ee and Ibn Maajah. Authenticated by al-Albaanee in *Saheeh al-Jaami'as-Sagheer*, vol.3, p.466, no.3767.

Allaah emphasized the importance of *Salaah* by making it the first of the various acts of worship which He made obligatory on Muslims. *Salaah* was made *Waajib* on Muslims while they were in Makkah before the *Hijrah* to al-Madeenah, while *Zakaah*, *Sawm* and *Hajj* only became *Waajib* on Muslims after they had emigrated to al-Madeenah. *Salaah* is also the first duty required of someone after he has declared his belief in Allaah and the Messenger (ﷺ). Allaah points to this fact saying,

إِنَّنِىٓ أَنَا ٱللَّهُ لَآ إِلَهَ إِلَّآ أَنَا۠ فَٱعۡبُدۡنِى وَأَقِمِ ٱلصَّلَوٰةَ لِذِكۡرِىٓ

"Verily I am Allaah, there is no other god beside Me, so worship Me alone and establish the *Salaah* in order to remember Me."

Soorah Taahaa (20) : 14

Allaah also stressed its importance by making it the first thing which we will be asked about on the Day of Judgement. This fact is recorded in the following statement of the Prophet (ﷺ): *"The first thing which a slave well be held to account for on the Day of Resurrection is* **Salaah**. *It if is good, all of the rest of his deeds become good, but if it is bad, all the rest of his deeds become bad."*[149] The Chapters of the Qur'aan are filled with references to *Salaah* as a basic Islamic practice repeated over and over again in various forms to emphasize its importance to Allaah. *Salaah* was so important to Allaah He personally informed the Prophet (ﷺ) about it being *Waajib* when the Prophet (ﷺ) travelled in the *Mi'raaj* above the heavens to be in direct contact with Allaah. Anas reported that *Salaah* was first made *Fard* during the Prophet's night journey fifty times (per day), but it was later decreased due to the Prophet's pleading until it reached five times with a reward for fifty.[150]

---

[149] Reported by Anas and collected by at-Tabaraanee in *al-Mu'jum al-Awsat* and authenticated by al-Albaanee in *Saheeh al-Jaami as-Sagheer*, vol.2, pp. 352-353, no.2570.

[150] Collected by Muslim (*Sahih Muslim* (English Trans.), vol.1, pp.103-104, no.313), Ahmad an-Nasaa'ee and at-Tirmithee.

It should also be noted that unlike the various other acts of worship which are obligatory for only certain categories of people or on particular occasions, such as *Zakaah* and *Hajj* being obligatory on the rich and *Sawm* being obligatory only one month out of the year, *Salaah* is obligatory on every adult five times per day throughout his life once he declares his *Eemaan*. Whether he is rich or poor, healthy or sick, travelling or at home, no one is excused from this obligation even on the battlefield a special form of *Salaah* has been prescribed.[151]

According to the law of Islaam, if someone stops praying and refuses to start back up again, he is classified as an apostate[152] and is executed so that his sickness doesn't spread in the society. Just as a cancerous organ is cut out of the body in order to save the remaining organs and the life of the individual, the life of the apostate is taken to save the life of the whole society. This clearly shows the serious attitude of Islaam towards *Salaah*.

THE BENEFITS OF SALAAH

Since *Salaah* is considered so important by Allaah and so essential to Islaam, and Allaah only demands of us things of benefit to us, let us now look at the need for *Salaah* and the benefits which we should gain from it:

1. Remembrance of Allaah

Since the majority of man's life is involved with worldly things like earning a living, eating, sleeping and social events, it is very easy for him to forget Allaah and his obligations to Him. When he forgets Allaah, the material things of this world fill up his life and his desires run wild trying to experience all of the pleasures, whether *Halaal* or *Haraam*. When he reaches this state of ignorance, he then begins to worship created things. Money becomes his god and becomes the goal of his

---

[151] The only exceptions being in the case of the woman on her menses or for a maximum of forty days after child birth, or for a person who became unconscious (he is not required to make up any *Salaah* that he missed while being unconscious).

[152] One who becomes a *Kaafir* after being Muslim.

life for which he would do anything. The little wealth which he has is squandered trying to fulfill his endless needs.

Because of this, Allaah placed a time for meditation and contemplation at five important points in man's day. The first thing in the morning before going go work, in the middle of the working day, in the mid-afternoon when work nears its end, after work in the early evening, and at night before he has to sleep. These periods take him out of the material world and remind him of Allaah and his relationship to Him. He is only a slave to Allaah and Allaah's pleasure is his goal. During these periods of remembrance, man is trained to remember Allaah so that when he goes about his daily life his mind remains on Allaah. This is why Allaah said,

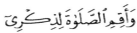

"And establish the _Salaah_ in order to remember Me."

Soorah Taahaa (20) : 14

2. Taqwaa: The Fear of Allaah

As the _Salaah_ helps man to remember Allaah, it also makes him aware that Allaah is watching his every move. There is no time when he is hidden from Allaah, even in the darkness and even when he is alone. He is never alone. He may be able to escape from all the punishments of the world, but he cannot escape from Allaah. _Taqwaa_ makes the believer alternate between the fear and love of Allaah. The believer fears displeasing Allaah, and so he carefully avoids the **Haraam**, _Makrooh_ and the _Mutashaabih_ and eagerly attempts to excel in the _Fard_, _Mustahabb_ and _Nafl_ [153] acts. The Prophet (ﷺ)said, "_The **Halaal** is clear and the **Haraam** is clear, and between them are doubtful matters unknown to most people. Whoever avoids the doubtful matters has protected his religion and his honour, and whoever falls into the doubtful matters (eventually) falls into the **Haraam**..._[154] It is this mixture of love and fear which compels him to observe the laws of Allaah in this life.

---

[153] Voluntary.

[154] Collected by al-Bukhaaree and Muslim. See _An-Nawawi's Forty Hadith_, p.42, no.6.

No matter how many laws are made and how many policemen and judges are hired to see that they are carried out, people only obey laws as long as they think that they can't get away with breaking them without being caught. But, once the opportunity to break the law appears, they don't hesitate to do so. For example, when there was a blackout in New York City for a few days in the summer of 1978, the whole city went wild. People, rich and poor alike, broke into stores and looted. The rich concentrated on jewelry stores, while the poor concentrated on furniture shops and department stores. The love and fear of Allaah is obviously far superior to the fear and respect of man-made laws because it governs the whole of a believer's life and makes a real change in his outlook. It is this quality of *Taqwaa* which makes the Muslim the only man capable of governing the earth and fulfilling the role of *Khaleefah* for which he was created.

3. Obedience and Control

The fact that we have to obey the call for prayer five times per day and line up behind the leader and follow him carefully, teaches us discipline and a respect for authority and leadership. Encouragement to cultivate the latter two qualities is a distinctive feature of the Islamic system. Abu Hurayrah quoted the Prophet (ﷺ) as saying, "*The **Imaam** was appointed to be followed, so do not differ from him. If he bows (**Rukoo'**), then bow; and if he says '**Sami' Allaahu liman hamidah**' (Allaah hears those who praise Him), then say, **Rabbanaa lakal-hamd** (Our Lord, all praise belongs to you)'; and if he prostrates (**Sujood**), prostrate after him...*"[155] The Prophet (ﷺ) was also reported to have said, "*A Muslim must listen to and obey his leader whether he likes it or not, as long as he is not commanded to do sin. If he is ordered to do sin, he should neither listen nor obey.*"[156] Everyone admires the discipline of the army and the order that it establishes. The purpose of their parade is to get them into the habit of carrying out orders. *Salaah* trains the believer in a similar fashion. It demands that he go through certain

---

[155] Collected by al-Bukhaaree (*Sahih al-Bukhari* (Arabic-English), vol.1, p.388, no.689) and Muslim.
[156] Collected by al-Bukhaaree (*Sahih al-Bukhari* (Arabic-English), vol.1, p.401, no.718).

specific motions, say certain specific statements, and to look at a particular spot. 'Aa'eshah said, *"I asked the Prophet (ﷺ) about looking around during prayer. He said, 'It is stolen property which Satan takes away from a person's prayer.'"*[157] All of the limbs of his body are put under strict control, and if control and discipline are broken, the whole *Salaah* has to be repeated. In some aspects the Islamic *Salaah* discipline is more rigid than the army because in *Salaah* we are not even allowed to break wind, while no such stipulation is placed on soldiers on parade. There is, however, a certain amount of flexibility in the orders to allow for the different abilities of people, thus making Islaam applicable everywhere. For instance, congregational *Salaah* is a requirement for men, but not so for women, as it would become a great burden for women, making it difficult for them to fulfill their obligations to the household. It is not advisable for the *Imaam* to make the recitation exceptionally long if he has minors and old people in his congregation. He also has to be careful about the interests of his congregation. Abu Hurayrah quoted the Prophet (ﷺ) as saying, *"If any of you leads the people in prayer, he should shorten it, for there are weak, sick and old among them. But if any of you prays alone, he may then prolong the prayer as much as he wishes."*[158] The Prophet (ﷺ) was also quoted as saying, *"(Sometimes) when I stand for prayer I intend to prolong it somewhat, but I hear the cries of a child so I shorten it in order to not trouble the mother."* If a person is sick and unable to make the *Salaah* in a standing position, he is allowed to do so in a sitting position, and even if this is not possible for him, then he is allowed to make *Salaah* in a lying position. These are only a few of the many examples indicating flexibility in the commands of *Salaah*. The army codes, on the other hand, are very rigid, so that only people whose bodies meet their requirements are allowed to participate.

The control and discipline which *Salaah* requires from the one performing it is designed to make him obey the divine commands between each *Salaah*. Just as he must control his eyes during *Salaah* by only

---

[157] Collected by al-Bukhaaree (*Sahih al-Bukhari* (Arabic English), vol.1, p.401, n.718).
[158] Collected by al-Bukhaaree (*Sahih al-Bukhari* (Arabic English), vol.1, p.379, no. 671).

looking at the place of *Sujood*, he must also control his eyes outside of *Salaah* by not looking at forbidden things like uncensored movies or peeping in private places. Similarly, his tongue and lips are trained in *Salaah* to say good things and to praise Allaah, so that he may avoid backbiting, slander and foul language when he is out of *Salaah*. His hands are put through controlled motions in *Salaah* so that he may control them from touching *Haraam* in his day to day life. He touches *Haraam* by stealing, by buying or selling what is *Haraam*, by eating or drinking what is *Haraam*, etc. Likewise, his feet are placed in specific places and bent in particular forms in order to train them in obedience to Allaah. Just as they are disciplined in *Salaah*, they must also be disciplined out of *Salaah* by not walking toward the *Haraam*, but walking away from it. This is the meaning of Allaah's statement.

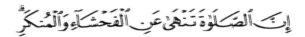

"Verily *Salaah* prevents (man from) evil speech and evil deeds."

Soorah al-'Ankaboot (29) : 45

4. Seeking Forgiveness

The Prophet (ﷺ) said, *"All of Aadam's descendants are forever making mistakes, but the best of those who make mistakes are those who seek forgiveness."*[159] This is the reality of man, no matter how righteous and good he may be, he is always falling into error. Of course the error of the righteous may not be like the ordinary people, but it is error nonetheless. Man is constantly in need of a means by which he may repent by asking Allaah's forgiveness and promising not to repeat the same or similar errors. Without any organized system which brings him in contact with Allaah regularly, he is liable to forget to seek repentance and may eventually lose even his feelings of guilt and choose the path of error. If he forgets to repent regularly, he could also feel that his sins are too many for Allaah to forgive and lose all hope of even getting back on the right path. So, *Salaah* provides an easy, regular means of

---

[159] Collected by Ibn Maajah, at-Tirmithee, Ahmad and ad-Daarimee. It is authenticated (*Hasan*) by al-Albanee in *Saheeh Sunan Ibn Maajah*, vol.2, p.418, no.3428.

seeking forgiveness and it keeps man constantly turning back to Allaah for help in overcoming his sinful ways. The believer never loses hope because he maintains a constant line of communication with his Lord.

SUBMISSIVENESS IN PRAYER

Khushoo' (humility or submissiveness) is a very important characteristic in *Salaah*, for Allaah says in the Qur'aan:

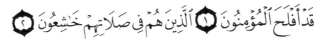

"Successful indeed are the Believers, those who humble themselves in their prayers."
Soorah al-Mu'minoon (23) : 1-2

To merely go throught the ritual of prayer will not help the believers to fulfill the obligations of prayer. For *Salaah* to be acceptable, it must proceed sincerely and fervently from the heart. This is possible through the believer attempting to fully concentrate on the supplications he utters in the various postures, by being conscious of His presence, by making sure that he is distanced from noise and by being physically comfortable by not being overly hungry or sleepy or suffering from the discomforts of weather. This is especially important in the posture of *Sujood*. A believer is closest to Allaah while in *Sujood*, and so it has been recommended to make extra *Du'aa* in this posture, for according to the *Hadeeth*, it is most likely to be answered. The believer's *Salaah* should be as if it is a farewell *Salaah*. The believer should feel in need of Allaah and as having totally surrendered himself to Him. In the words of the Qur'aan, the believer should be able to proclaim:

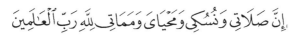

"Verily, my prayer and my service of sacrifice, my life and my death are all for Allaah, Lord of the Worlds."
Soorah al-An'aam (6) : 162

He should feel lowly and insignificant before His Majesty, as the Prophet (ﷺ) related, *"He who has in his heart a mustard seed of pride would not enter Paradise."*

One cannot be smug about one's prayers and deeds; There is always room for improvement and one must look up to those who are better than him in these areas. *Khushoo'* is achieved throught feelings of gratitude for the many blessings Allaah has granted and by feeling obliged to be helpful to the needy; by a reflective scanning of one's deeds and intentions with a heart fervently repentant about the errors one has made. Submissiveness in prayer comes to the believer who remembers the reality of the end of this life in the form of the Day of Judgement, about its just rewards and terrible punishment. It comes through attempting to devoutly follow the way of the Prophet (ﷺ) and his companions (*Sunnah*). It comes to those who try to fortify their faith by remembering Allaah a lot, by making voluntary prayers, through recitation of the Qur'aan and *Thikr,* thus trying to evade Satan, who attempts to distract us in our *Salaah.* And it comes to those who seek Allaah's help for it by supplicating:

$$رَبِّ ٱجۡعَلۡنِى مُقِيمَ ٱلصَّلَوٰةِ وَمِن ذُرِّيَّتِى رَبَّنَا وَتَقَبَّلۡ دُعَآءِ$$

"O Lord! Make me and my offspring of those who establish regular *Salaah.* O our Lord, and accept my supplication."

Soorah Ibraaheem (14) : 40

CATEGORIES OF SALAAH

Salaah may be divided into three main categories: *Fard, Sunnah* and *Nafl.*

Fard

These prayers are the compulsory five: *Fajr, Thuhr, 'Asr, Maghrib* and *'Eshaa',* about which the Prophet (ﷺ) said, *"Allaah has prescribed five daily prayers for His slaves. For whoever does them without losing any due to neglect, Allaah has promised to put him in Paradise."* Also amongst the *Fard Salaah* are *Jumu'ah.*

162

Sunnah

They are the various _Salaahs_ which the Prophet (ﷺ) recommended that we do:

Al-'Eidayn: The _Salaahs_ performed at the end of _Ramadaan_ ('Eid al-Fitr_) and on the 10th of _Thul-Hijjah_ ('Eid al-Ad-haa_).

Al-Kusoof and al-Khusoof: _Al-Kusoof_ is the _Salaah_ done during a solar eclipse, and _al-Khusoof_ is the _Salaah_ done during, a lunar eclipse. The Prophet (ﷺ) said, _"The sun and the moon are two signs of Allaah; They are not eclipsed for the death or birth of anyone. When you see one of them eclipsed, you should make **Du'aa** to Allaah and make **Salaah** until the eclipse ends."_[160]

Al-Istisqaa: The _Salaah_ done to seek rain in times of drought.

Tahiyyatul-Masjid: They are the two _Raka'aat_ performed when someone enters a _Masjid_. They should be done before he sits down. The Prophet (ﷺ) said, " _If one of you enters the Masjid, he should not sit until he has offered two **Raka'aat**._"[161]

Al-Wudoo': Two _Raka'aat_ done after the completion of _Wudoo'_. The Prophet (ﷺ) said, _"Whoever does two **Raka'aat** (regularly) sincerely after making **Wudoo'** properly will enter Paradise."_[162]

Ad-Duhaa: Two or more _Raka'aat_ done after the rising of the sun. They are also known as _Salaah al-Ishraaq_.

At-Taraweeh: Eleven _Raka'aat_ done after _Salaah al-'Eshaa'_ during _Ramadaan_.

---

[160] Collected by al-Bukhaaree (_Sahih al-Bukhari_ (Arabic-English), vol.2, p. 96, no.168) and Muslim (_Sahih al-Muslim_ (English Trans.), vol.2, p.433, no.1987).

[161] Collected by al-Bukhaaree (_Sahih al-Bukhari_ (Arabic-English), vol.1, p.259, no.435), Muslim (_Sahih Muslim_ (English Trans), vol.1, p.347, no.540) and Abu Daawood (_Sunan Abu Dawud_ (English Trans.), vol.1, p.120, no.467).

[162] Collected by Muslim (_Sahih Muslim_ (English Trans.), vol.1, p.152, no.451).

Ar-Rawaatib: The *Raka'aat* done before and after the five *Fard Salaahs*. The purpose of these *Raka'aat* are basically two: (1) to prepare one for the *Fard*, and (2) to make up for any weakness in the *Fard*.

Nafl

These are the *Salaahs* which can be done at anytime during the day or night except for the prohibited times (after *Salaah al-Fajr* until the sunrise, during sunrise, when the sun reaches its zenith, after *Salaah al-'Asr* until sunset, and during the setting of the sun). They are extra *Salaah* done by choice and have not been specified by the Prophet (ﷺ) (e.g. extra *Salaah* done after *Sunan Salaah*).

SALAAH AL-JAMAA'AH (CONGREGATIONAL SALAAH)

All of the *Fard Salaahs* and some of the *Sunnah Salaahs* are made to be performed as a group and not individually. The Prophet (ﷺ) stressed the superiority of the group *Salaah* by saying, *"Verily **Salaah al-Jamaa'ah** is better than the individual **Salaah** by twenty-seven degrees."[163]*

The Purpose of Salaah al-Jamaa'ah

The main purpose is to develop in the minds and the hearts of the believers an understanding of the importance of the group effort in fulfilling Allaah's commands. Allaah not only commands us as individuals to submit to and obey Him, but he also ordered us to make the rest of the world submit to His laws and obey them. The fulfilment of our role as *Khaleefah*, (Inheritors of the earth), only takes place when the *Sharee'ah* (Allaah's law) is propagated and enforced in the world, and the laws of *Shaytaan* are abolished. This great duty, which Allaah has placed on each and every one of us, cannot be performed individually. It has to be done as a group and in an organized fashion. *Salaah* in congregation trains individual Muslims and prepares them to take up that mighty task as a unified body of believers.

---

[163] Collected by al-Bukhaaree (*Sahih al-Bukhari* (Arabic-English), vol.1,p.351, no.618). Muslim (*Sahih Muslim* (English Trans.), vol.1, p.314, no.1360) and Abu Daawood (*Sunan Abu Dawud* (English Trans.), vol.1, p.147, no.559).

The Benefits of Salaah al-Jamaa'ah

Awareness: Salaah in *Jamaa'ah* helps us develop an awareness of our fellow Muslims, which is encouraged according to the Islamic principle that the Muslim nation is like parts of the same body. An-Nu'maan ibn Basheer quoted the Prophet (ﷺ) as saying, *"The believers in regard to their mutual love, affection and concern are like one body: when any limb aches, the whole body aches due to sleeplessness and fever."*[164] Prayer in congregation brings us in contact with our brothers and makes us aware of their condition. When we see others who are disabled or wearing tattered clothes, we are urged to try and help them in whatever way we can. Also, when a brother is absent, it develops concern in those who usually pray with him so that they may visit him if he is sick or hurt, or help out his family if he has died.

Equality and Brotherhood: Since all must stand shoulder to shoulder in rows, without any reserved places, the congregational *Salaah* confirms the brotherhood and equality of Islaam. The rich and poor, noble and common are all equal before Allaah. Even the position of the Imaam is not the birthright of any special class, but the duty of the most knowledgeable among the community.

Unity and Strength: Standing in lines, making the same movements, speaking and thinking similar words and thoughts help to develop a singleness of purpose in the minds of the believers. It produces a spiritual unity which is an important part of the bond which cements the brotherhood together. Abu Moosaa related that the Prophet (ﷺ) said, *"A believer to another believer is like a building, each part strengthening the other."* The Prophet (ﷺ) *then clasped his hands together with his fingers interlaced.*[165]

---

[164] Collected by al-Bukhaaree (*Sahih al-Bukhari* (Arabic-English), vol.8, p.34, no.55) and Muslim.
[165] Collected by al-Bukhaaree and Muslim (*Sahih Muslim* (English Trans.), vol.4, p. 1368, no.6258).

Missing the Jamaa'ah

Because of the importance of the _Salaah al-Jamaa'ah_ in Islaam, ne-glecting it is bordering on sin. The Prophet (ﷺ) himself emphasized how serious this form of negligence is by saying, _"By the One in Whose Hands my soul lies, I had decided to have firewood gathered and the A_th_aan for **Salaah** made. Then I would have a man lead the people in **Salaah** and I would go and set on fire the houses of those who didn't attend the _Salaah_."_[166] Ibn 'Abbaas had also said that " There is no _Salaah_ for one who hears the call (to prayer) and doesn't come, except if he has a good reason like sickness."[167] Therefore, we are obliged to make every effort to make our _Fard Salaah_ in _Jamaa'ah_ as much as possible and encourage our family and friends to do the same.

Method of Joining the Jamaa'ah

At whatever point one joins the congregation, the _Takbeeratul-Ihraam_ has to be made to enter _Salaah_. Then follow the _Imaam_ at whatever point he is in. If one joins before the _Imaam_ has risen from the _Rukoo'_, then one is not required to make up the _Rak'ah_. Any other _Raka'aats_ missed must be made up after the _Imaam_ pronounces _Tasleem_. If, how-ever, the _Imaam_ follows up the _Tasleem_ with _Sujood as-Sahw_ and one has already risen, one has the choice to continue or to follow the _Imaam_, though the latter is preferrable.

The _Imaam_ can be corrected if he makes an error in _Salaah_. If the error is in the recitation, the correction is made by reciting the correct verse. If the error is in actions, it is made by saying "_Subhaan Allaah_" to notify him of the error.[168]

---

[166] Reported by Abu Hurayrah and collected by al-Bukhaaree (_Sahih al-Bukhari_ (Arabic-English), vol.1, pp.350-351, no.617) and Muslim (_Sahih Muslim_ (English Trans.), vol.1, p.316, no.

[167] Collected by Abu Daawood (_Sunan Abu Dawud_ (English Trans.), vol.1, p.145, no.551), Ibn Maajah and Ibn Hibbaan.

[168] One can offer one's obligatory prayer with someone praying a _Nafl_ prayer, even if the number of _Raka'aats_ the _Imaam_ is offering is less than the latter.

QUESTIONS

1. Give the literal and Islamic meanings of _Salaah_.

2. Two reasons why Salaah is considered the most important form of worship in Islaam are
> (a) it is the first thing that we will be questioned about on the Last Day, and after _Zakaah_, it was the first pillar to be made compulsory on the Muslims.
> (b) the Prophet (ﷺ) said that if one stops praying, he falls into _Kufr_, and it will be the first thing that we will be questioned about on the Last Day.
> (c) the command for _Salaah_ came right after the _Hijrah_ to Madeenah and it is the first duty required of a Muslim after declaring his faith.
> (d) _Salaah_ is obligatory on everyone in every situation, while the other pillars are optional, and the Prophet (ﷺ) stressed the importance of _Salaah_ by saying that "_Between a man and disbelief is Salaah._"
> (e) it is the first duty required of a Muslim after declaring his faith and it is the last thing that we will be questioned about on the Last Day.

3. The Islamic punishment for one who quits making _Salaah_ and refuses to start again is just because
> (a) people who are too lazy to pray can be of no benefit to the society.
> (b) it is better for a person committing such a serious sin to be executed so that they cannot continue sinning and have to answer for more bad deeds on the Last Day.
> (c) it prevents him from having any harmful effects on the society.
> (d) it prevents others from having doubts about the importance of prayer.
> (e) a person who quits praying may eventually quit fasting and giving _Zakaah_, which are the most important pillars of Islaam.

4. Briefly summarize the four main benefits of *Salaah*.

5. The three main categories of *Salaah* are
    (a) *Fard, Jamaa'ah* and *Nafl.*
    (b) *Fard, Sunnah* and *Jamaa'ah.*
    (c) *Waajib, Mubaah* and *Nafl.*
    (d) *Fard, Sunnah* and *Nafl.*
    (e) *Waajib, Sunnah* and *Fard.*

18. FIQH: SUJOOD AS-SAHW

The Meaning of Sujood as-Sahw

Sujood is the plural of *Sajdah*, which means prostration, or putting one's head, hands, knees and toes and the ground. *Sahw* means to forget. Therefore, *Sujood as-Sahw* means the prostrations for forgetfulness. Islamically, it refers to two *Sajdahs* made at the end of *Salaah* to make up for major errors during *Salaah*.

The Background of Sujood as-Sahw

Since human beings are by nature forgetful, it is not surprising that even when they are praying to God, they may forget something. Allaah was well aware of this fact, so He had Prophet Muhammad (ﷺ) forget a few times in his *Salaah*, then correct it so that he could show all the Muslims till the end of time exactly how they should correct the mistakes which they make in their prayers. The Prophet (ﷺ) used to make two *Sajdahs* at the end of his *Salaah* if he made a big mistake in his *Salaah*.

The Reason of Sujood

There is a reason why Allaah had us make *Sajdah* in order for us to correct our mistakes and not *Rukoo'* or *Qiyaam*. If we think deeply about it we will realize that the main reason why we forget things in *Salaah* is because *Shaytaan* fills our minds with foolish thoughts and causes us to do so. Or, maybe our desires have defeated us and we have obeyed them by thinking about what we want to do after our *Salaah*, etc. Therefore, the best way to make up is to bow down to Alllaah, glorify Him and ask His forgiveness, since the greatest act of submission is the act of prostration.

The Significance of Sujood as-Sahw

1. This way of making up for our mistakes is really a great mercy from Allaah because He could have had us repeat the whole *Salaah* from beginning to end for every mistake, in which case we might never be

able to stop praying since none of us can pray a perfect _Salaah_. Instead, Allaah has only required us to make two _Sajdahs_ to cover up for our mistakes.

2. _Sujood as-Sahw_ shows that Islaam is a very practical religion which takes into account human weaknesses and provides easy means of correcting them.

Circumstances in Which Sujood as-Sahw is Required

There are two main occasions when _Sujood as-Sahw_ is required:

1. When one adds or subtracts anything of great importance to or from the acts of _Salaah_.

> _Examples of Additions_: Praying 5 _Raka'aat_ instead of 4, doing three prostrations instead or 2, or making _Tashahhud_ at the end of the first _Rak'ah_.
> _Examples of Subtractions_: Praying 3 _Raka'aat_ instead of 4, doing one _Sajdah_ instead of two, or getting up for the third _Rak'ah_ without making _Tashahhud_.

2. When one forgets the number of _Raka'aat_, being in doubt as to whether one is in the third or fourth _Rak'ah_ etc.

The Time for Sujood as-Sahw

The Sujood can be done at two possible times in _Salaah_: (1) It can be done immediately before _Tasleem_ (saying "_Assalaamu 'alaykum_") at the end of the _Salaah_, or (2) it can be done after the _Tasleem_.

Method of Sujood as-Sahw

This _Sujood_ can be done in the following two ways:

1. After completing the first and second _Tashahhud_ (i.e. "_Attahiyyaatu lil-laahi.._" and "_Allaahumma Salli 'alaa Muhammad..._") and seeking refuge from the five trials ("_Allaahumma innee a'oothu bika min athaabi_

jahannam..") we say *"Allaahu akbar,"* then make the first *Sajdah.* In *Sajdah* we say the usual *Du'aa (Subhana rabbiyal-aa'laa)* three times, then make *Takbeer* (i.e. say *"Allaahu akbar")* and return to *Jalsah* (the sitting position), where we also say our usual *Du'aa ("Allaahumma maghfirlee warhamnee...").* We again make *Takbeer* and bow down in the second *Sajdah* where we make the same *Du'aa* as before. We then make *Takbeer* for the last time, return to *Jalsah* and turn our heads to the right and left making *Tasleem.*

2. In the second form, we continue our <u>S</u>alaah all the way to *Tasleem,* after which we make *Takbeer* and prostrate in our first *Sajdah,* saying the usual *Du'aa* of *Sajdah.* We then make *Takbeer* and do our second *Sajdah,* saying the usual *Du'aa.* Finally, we make the last *Takbeer* and return to *Jalsah,* where we either make *Tasleem* immediately or make *Tashahhud* again and then make *Tasleem.*

Method of Correction

1. If we realize before making *Tasleem* that we have added anything to the <u>S</u>alaah, for example and extra *Rak'ah,* we may make the two *Sujood as-Sahw* before or after *Tasleem.*

2. If we realize after *Tasleem* that we added something, we just make our *Sujood as-Sahw* as soon as we find out.

3. If we leave out any of the main actions or sayings of <u>S</u>alaah, such as the *Tashahhud* or a *Sajdah,* we simply make the two prostrations for forgetfulness before the *Tasleem* or after.

4. If we leave out one or more whole *Rak'ahs,* we must get up and complete them, then at the end we should make the *Sujood as-Sahw* before or after the *Tasleem.*

5. If we forget to make *Sujood as-Sahw* before the *Tasleem,* we simply make it after *Tasleem.*

6. If the Imaam makes a mistake, he is required to make *Sujood as-Sahw* and we all must follow him.

7. If we make a mistake while praying behind him, we are not allowed to make *Sujood as-Sahw* because the Prophet (ﷺ) said, *"Verily the Imaam was made to be followed."*[169]

---

[169] Collected by al-Bukhaaree (<u>Sahih</u> al-Bukhari (Arabic-English), vol.1, p.388, no.689) and Muslim (<u>Sahih</u> Muslim (English Trans.), vol.1, p.226, no.817).

8. If, however, we joined the _Salaah_ late and made a mistake in the part of our _Salaah_ which we are making up, we then have to make _Sujood as-Sahw_ to correct it.

QUESTIONS

1. Islamically, *Sujood as-Sahw* refers to
    (a) forgetfulness.
    (b) the errors made in *Salaah*.
    (c) two prostrations made in *Salaah*.
    (d) two *Sajdahs* made at the end of *Salaah* for errors made in *Salaah*.
    (e) prostrations that were missed earlier.

2. *Sujood as-Sahw* is required on two main occasions:
    (a) when something has been subtracted or multiplied in Salaah and when the number of *Raka'aat* is doubtful.
    (b) whenever anything occurs to the *Salaah* to increase or decrease its actions or sayings.
    (c) when something major has been added or dropped from the *Salaah*, and when the number of *Raka'aat* has been forgotten.
    (d) if there is a decrease or increase in the major acts of *Salaah*.
    (e) if one forgets which Rak'ah he is in or if one adds an act to the *Salaah*.

3. If someone adds an extra *Rukoo'* to the *Salaah*, the error should be corrected by
    (a) making a *Sajdah* after the *Tasleem*.
    (b) making two *Sajdahs* before the *Tasleem*.
    (c) adding two prostrations, one before the *Tasleem* and one after.
    (d) performing two prostrations after the *Tasleem*.
    (e) doing a *Sajdah* before the *Tasleem*.

4. If one makes a major mistake while praying behind and *Imaam*, he should
    (a) make two *Sajdahs* after the *Tasleem*.
    (b) do two *Sajdahs* before the *Tasleem*.
    (c) pray an extra *Rak'ah* after the *Tasleem*.
    (d) add two extra *Raka'aat* after the *Tasleem*.
    (e) none of the above.

19. FIQH: QADAA (MAKING UP)

Definition

Qadaa is the act of performing *Salaah* after its stipulated time because it was not done, whether intentionally or unintentionally.

Method

If someone slept through the time frame of the *Salaah* of *Fajr*, for example, he should upon awakening make *Wudoo'*, then make the *Iqaamah* and perform the *Salaah* just as he would have if he were doing it on time. Abu Qataadah said, *"One night during a journey with the Prophet (ﷺ), some people said, 'If only the Prophet (ﷺ) would take rest with us during the last hours of the night.' He replied, 'I am afraid that you will sleep and miss the Fajr (morning) prayer.' Bilaal said, 'I will awaken you.' So they all slept, and Bilaal leaned against his mount and fell asleep. The Prophet (ﷺ) woke up when the sun began to rise and said, 'O Bilaal, what happened to your statement?' He replied, 'I have never slept so much before!' The Prophet (ﷺ) said, 'Allaah took our souls when He wished and released them when He wished. O Bilaal, get up and call the **Athaan** for prayer.' The Prophet (ﷺ) then made **Wudoo'** and when the sun came up completely he stood up and prayed."*[170]

Time Period

(a) One who misses *Salaah* is responsible for it and should perform it whenever he remembers or is able, even if it was missed years ago. Ibraaheem said, *"One who missed a prayer twenty years ago need only pray that single prayer."*[171] Anas quoted the Prophet (ﷺ) as saying, *"If anyone misses a prayer, he should pray it when he remembers it. There*

---

[170] Collected by al-Bukhaaree (*Sahih al-Bukhari* (Arabic-English), vol.1 1, p.327, no.569)
[171] Collected by al-Bukhaaree (*Sahih al-Bukhari* (Arabic-English), vol.1, p.328, Chapter (37).

is no expiation except the prayer itself.."[172] To miss *Salaah* deliber-
ately is an act of disbelief, so it is necessary to repent prior to making
up missed prayers.

(b) If, for example, the *Salaah* of *Thuhr* was missed and one remember
at the time of the *Salaah* of 'Asr, he should perform it either before or
after the *Salaah* of 'A*s*r.

(c) If the *Iqaamah* for the *Salaah* of 'Asr is made before he can make
his *Thuhr*, he should delay it until after the *Salaah* of 'A*s*r is complete.
The Prophet (ﷺ) has said, "*If the Iqaamah is made, the only acceptable* **Salaah** *is the* **Fard Salaah***.*"[173]

---

[172]   Collected by al-Bukhaaree (*Sahih al-Bukhari* (Arabic-English), vol.1, p.328,
no.571).
[173]   Collected by Muslim (*Sahih Muslim* (English Trans.) vol.1, p.345, no.1531.).

QUESTIONS

1. Islamically, *Qadaa* refers to
    (a) the joining of two *Salaahs*.
    (b) the shortening of a four *Raka'aat Salaah* to two *Raka'aat*.
    (c) the praying of a *Salaah* before its time along with the *Salaah* which proceeds it.
    (d) the making up of a missed prayer.
    (e) the making up for errors in a missed *Salaah*.

2. If someone misses *Salaah al-Fajr* and prays it just before the *Athaan* of *Thuhr*, it is considered as
    (a) prayed on time.
    (b) a missed *Salaah* which will have to be made up later.
    (c) *Qadaa*.
    (d) a late *Salaah* after which two *Sajdahs* for forgetfulness will have to be made.
    (e) *Jama' Salaah*.

3. If someone did not pray the recommended two units of *Sunnah* prayer before the compulsory units of *Salaah al-Fajr* and the *Iqaamah* was called,
    (a) he should quickly pray the two units of *Sunnah*, then join the congregation for the *Fard* of *Fajr*.
    (b) he should join the congregation for the *Fard* of *Fajr*.
    (c) he may make *Qadaa* for them before praying *Salaah al-Fajr*.
    (d) he cannot pray *Salaah al-Fajr* until he has prayed the two units.
    (e) he may join the congregation for *Salaah al-Fajr* after performing the two recommended units of *Sunnah*.

20. FIQH: MAS-H

Definition

Islamically, *Mas-h* refers to the act of wiping ones wet hands on one's hair, or on one's turban instead of one's hair; and one's socks or shoes instead of washing the feet during *Wudoo'*.

Conditions for Wiping on Socks and Shoes

The wiping of socks or shoes can only take place if the following three conditions are met:

1. The sock or shoe had to have been put on after the foot was washed for a previous *Wudoo'*.
2. The sock or shoe should cover the whole foot up to and including the ankle.
3. One must still be within the allowed time period for wiping.

Time Period

The resident is allowed to perform *Mas-h* for a period of twenty-four hours, while the traveller is allowed to do so for seventy-two hours (i.e. three days).[174] Once the time period ends, a new *Wudoo'* can only made if the socks or shoes are removed and the feet washed.

Points of Note

(a)   If one still has *Wudoo'* at the end of the time period, he is not automatically required to renew is *Wudoo'* until he breaks it.
(b)   The time period begins when the socks or shoes are first wiped.
(c)   The acts which break *Wudoo'*[175] with *Mas-h* are the same as those with regular *Wudoo'*.

---

[174]   Collected by Muslim (*Sahih Muslim* (English Trans.), vol.1, p.165, no.537) and Abu Daawood (*Sunan Abu Dawud* (English Trans.), vol.1, p.38, no.157). Note: A mistake was made in typesetting the English version of this *Hadeeth* in *Sunan Abu Dawud.*

[175]   For example if *Wudoo'* is broken by a wet dream, the socks would have to be removed for *Wudoo'* to be regained by making a *Ghusl* (ritual bath).

(d)   If the socks or shoes are removed and *Wudoo'* is broken, the feet must be washed and a new time period starts.

(e)   It is not a requirement that one be sick or in difficulty to make *Mas-h*.

Method

The correct method of performing *Mas-h* is to pass one's wet hands over the tops of the socks or shoes and not the bottoms. 'Alee ibn Abee Taalib said, "*If the religion was simply logic, the bottoms of the Khuffs (leather socks) should be wiped instead of the tops, but I saw Allaah's Messenger wipe the top and not the bottom.*"[176] It doesn't matter whether one passes the left hand over his right foot and vice versa, or if he uses his right hand for both or his left hand for both.

---

[176] Collected by Abu Daawood (*Sunan Abu Dawud*) (English Trans.), vol.1, p.40, no.162).

QUESTIONS

1. *Mas-h* can only be performed by
  (a) Someone who is in poor health.
  (b) a traveller until he returns home.
  (c) a sick person for 72 hours and a healthy person for 24.
  (d) someone wearing shoes or socks which cover the knees.
  (e) one who washed his feet for a previous *Wudoo'* before wearing his socks.

2. The time period in which *Mas-h* may be done is
  (a) 27 hours for a resident and 42 hours for a traveller.
  (b) 72 hours for a resident and 24 hours for a traveller.
  (c) 42 hours for a resident and 72 hours for a traveller.
  (d) 24 hours for a resident and 82 hours for a traveller.
  (e) 24 hours for a resident and 72 hours for a traveller

3. *Mas-h* is correctly done by wiping one's wet hands on
  (a) the tops and bottoms of one's socks at the same time.
  (b) the bottoms of one's socks and not the tops.
  (c) on the tops of one's socks and not the bottoms.
  (d) on the bottoms of the socks before the tops.
  (e) the bottoms of the socks, wiping the right sock first.

21. FIQH: QASR (SHORTENING) AND JAMA' (JOINING)

Definition

Qasr is the shortening of a four *Raka'aat Salaah* to two *Raka'aat*, and *Jama'* is the praying of *Salaah ath-Thuhr* and *Salaah al-'Asr* together or *Salaah al-Maghrib* and *Salaah al-'Eshaa'* together.

Conditions

(a) *Qasr* can only be performed by one who is travelling. There is no time limit as long as he has not returned home.

(b) *Jama'* can be performed by the traveller as well as the resident under certain circumstances.

(c) In the case of bad weather conditions, *Salaah* in the Masjid may be joined.

(d) In the case of sicknesses like a weak bladder, one may also join *Salaahs*.

(e) The *Salaah* of *Fajr* cannot be joined to either *al-'Eshaa'* or *ath-Thuhr*, nor can the *Salaahs* of *'Asr* and *Maghrib* be joined with each other.

Method

Jama' Salaah may be performed in two ways:

(a) *Jama' Taqdeem (advanced combination)*

This is when the *Salaah* of *'Asr* is prayed in advance with that of *Thuhr* in the time of *Thuhr*, or when the *Salaah* of *'Eshaa'* is prayed in advance with *al-Maghrib* in the time of *Maghrib*.

(b) *Jama' Takheer (delayed combination)*

This is when the *Salaah* of *Thuhr* is delayed and prayed with that of *'Asr* in the time of *'Asr*, or when the *Salaah* of *Maghrib* is delayed and prayed with *al-Eshaa'* in the time of *'Eshaa'*. The *Salaahs* are joined by making one *Athaan* and two *Iqaamahs*. The *Athaan* is called, then the *Iqaamah* immediately after it. The first *Salaah* is prayed, and the second *Iqaamah* and *Salaah* are then made immediately after the *Tasleem* of the first *Salaah*.

Points of Note

(a)   If a resident prays behind a travelling *Imaam* who is making *Qasr*, the resident must get up and complete the remaining two *Rak'aat* after the *Imaam's Tasleem*.

(b)   A traveller praying behind a resident *Imaam* must complete the four *Rak'aat* and is not allowed to make *Qasr* even if he joins the *Salaah* in the third *Rak'aah*.

QUESTIONS

1. *Qasr Salaah* can only be done by
    (a) one who is making *Qadaa*.
    (b) shortening the prayers by one-half.
    (c) one who is sick or crippled.
    (d) a resident praying behind a travelling *Imaam*.
    (e) a traveller.

2. *Jama' Salaah* is performed by
    (a) only a traveller.
    (b) a traveller only when he does *Qasr*.
    (c) one wearing shoes or socks above the ankles.
    (d) a resident only in the case of illness, bad weather or real need.
    (e) one who made *Wudoo'* before putting on his socks.

22. FIQH: HAJJ

Definition

Hajj can also be pronounced "_Hijj_," and they both mean literally to head for a place. Islamically, both are names for the pilgrimage to Makkah in a state of _Ihraam_ during the months of _Hajj_ and the performance of certain religious rites there according to the method defined by the Prophet (ﷺ).

THE PREREQUISITES FOR HAJJ BEING WAAJIB

Hajj is _Waajib_ (compulsory) on Muslims according to the Qur'aan and the _Sunnah_. Allaah states in the Qur'aan,

And pilgrimage to the House is a duty unto Allaah for him among mankind who can find a way there."

Soorah Aal-'Imraan (3) : 97

Ibn 'Umar narrated that the Prophet (ﷺ) said, "_Islaam is based on five (pillars): bearing witness that there is no God besides Allaah and that Muhammad is His servant and messenger, establishing Salaah, paying Zakaah, fasting in Ramadaan and pilgrimage to Allaah's House._"[177]

The individual who is required to make _Hajj_ is one who is: (1) Muslim, (2) past puberty, (3) sane, and (4) able (monetarily[178] and physically). 'Alee ibn Abee Taalib reported that the Prophet (ﷺ) stated, "_The pen is raised from (the record book) of three people: the one who is asleep_

---

[177] Collected by al-Bukhaaree (_Sahih al-Bukhari_ (Arabic-English), vol.1, p.17, no.7) and Muslim (_Sahih Muslim_ (English Trans.), vol.1, pp.9-10, no.18).
[178] It is not a condition that one's female dependents of marriageable age be married before one sets out for _Hajj_.

until he awakes, the child until he becomes a youth, and the insane until he regains his sanity."[179]

TYPES OF HAJJ

There are three types of *Hajj* that one can perform.

1. Hajj Ifraad

This form of *Hajj* is done without sacrifice and doesn't have an *'Umrah* with it. It is *Hajj* by itself.

2. Hajj Qiraan

This form is for one who brings with him a sacrificial animal. He performs the rites of *'Umrah*, but remains in *Ihraam*[180] until the eighth of *Thul-Hijjah* (i.e. the first day of *Hajj*), then sets off-for Minaa to perform the rites of *Hajj* in the same *Ihraam*. He is required to sacrifice the animal he brought with him.

3. Hajj Tamattu'

This form is for one who intends to make *'Umrah* first, then *Hajj*. He first performs *'Umrah*, then discards his *Ihraam* on its completion. On the first day of *Hajj* he puts on his *Ihraam* again and sets out for Minaa. He is also required to buy an animal and sacrifice it on the day of sacrifice.

THE FAREWELL PILGRIMAGE OF THE MESSENGER OF ALLAAH (ﷺ)

When Jaabir ibn 'Abdullaah died in Madeenah at the age of ninety, he was the last living companion of the Prophet (ﷺ). Some time before

---

[179] Collected by Abu Daawood (*Sunan Abu Dawud* (English Trans), vol.3, p.1227, no.4389), at-Tirmithee (authenticated in *Saheeh Sunan at-Tirmithee*, vol.2, p.64, no.1150) and Ibn Maajah (authenticated in *Saheeh Sunan ibn Maajah*, vol.1, p.347, no.1660).

[180] *Ihraam* is the wearing of two sheets of cloth in the case of men, and garments which a woman chooses to wear, with the intention of performing either *'Umrah* or *Hajj* or both together.

his death, Muhammad ibn 'Alee, the grandson of Husayn, went to see him, along with a few of his companions. Muhammad ibn 'Alee said that when he disclosed his identity to Jaabir, the latter was very delighted. Jaabir wished God's blessing on him and welcomed him to his place, and then invited him to ask what he had come to ask.

Muhammad reported that when he began asking questions, the time for prayer approached, Jaabir then put on a short cloak of his and stood up for the prayer. The cloak was so short that it would slip down over and over again, but he completed the prayer in it, though he had a larger one lying on a clothing rack nearby. After the prayer, Muhammad asked him narrate the complete details of the Farewell Pilgrimage of the Messenger of Allaah (ﷺ).

Jaabir counted nine on his finger and said that the Prophet (ﷺ) did not go for *Hajj* during the first nine years of his stay at Madeenah. Then in the tenth year after the *Hijrah* (migration to Madeenah), he publicly announced that he would be going for *Hajj* that year. People started pouring into Madeenah from everywhere in order to accompany the Prophet (ﷺ) to Makkah and learn the correct method of *Hajj* directly from him. The *Hajj* caravan moved out from the city headed by the Prophet (ﷺ) and halted at Thul-Hulayfah, for a day or so. During the stay at Thul-Hulayfah, Asmaa' bint 'Umais, a wife of Abu Bakr, gave birth to Muhammad ibn Abu Bakr. Asmaa' then asked the Prophet (ﷺ), through a messenger, what she should do. The Prophet (ﷺ) sent a message back to her that she should bathe, put a cloth pad on her private parts and put on the *Ihraam* (clothes for *Hajj*).

After leading the prayer at Thul-Hulayfah, the Prophet (ﷺ) mounted his camel called Qaswaa and rode to a nearby elevated plain called Baydaa'. When Jaabir looked around in all directions as far as he could see, there were multitudes of people, some riding and some on foot. Jaabir said, "The Messenger of Allaah was in our midst, and since he was receiving revelation, we followed him in whatever he did." Here, at Baydaa', the Prophet (ﷺ) recited the following *Talbeeyah* aloud:

(*Labbayk, Allaahumma Labbayk! Labbaykaa, laa shareeka laka labbayk. Inaal-hamda wan-n' imata laka wal-mulk, laa shareeka lak*) "Here I am, O Allaah, here I am! You have no partner; here I am! You alone deserve all praise and gratitude! To you alone belong all favours, blessings and sovereignty and you have no partner."

The companions also recited their *Talbeeyahs* aloud adding a few words, but the Prophet (ﷺ) did not mind the additions, he just went on reciting his own *Talbeeyah*. Jaabir went on to say, "The main purpose of our journey was to accomplish *Hajj* and not *'Umrah*, so when we reached the House of Allaah, the Prophet (ﷺ) kissed the Black Stone and then started walking around the *Ka'bah*. He completed the first three circuits at a swift pace and the last four at a normal walking pace. Then he came to the place of Abraham (*Maqaam Ibraaheem*) and recited the following verse:

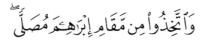

"Wattakhithoo mim-maqaami Ibraaheema musallaa." (Dedicate for prayer the place where Abraham stood. [2:125])

He then stood up for prayer with the place of Abraham between him and the *Ka'bah* and offered two *Raka'aat* (units of prayer) in which he recited *Qulyaa ayyuhal-kaafiroon* (109) and *Qul huwallaahu ahad* (112). Then he returned to the Black Stone, kissed it, and went out through a gate towards Mt. Safaa. When he reached it, he recited,

إِنَّ ٱلصَّفَا وَٱلْمَرْوَةَ مِن شَعَآئِرِ ٱللَّهِ

"Innas-Safaa wal-Marwata min sha'aa'irillaah." (Indeed Safaa and Marwah are among the signs of Allaah [2:158])

Then he said, *"I begin my Sa'yi from Safaa since Allaah mentioned it before Marwah.'* He then climbed Mt. Safaa till he could clearly see the House of Allaah and stood facing it while declaring the oneness and Greatness of Allaah and saying,

(Laa illaha il-lal-laah wahdahu laa shareeka lah, lahul-mulk wa lahul hamd wa huwa 'ala kulli shay'in Qadeer. Laa illaha il-lal-laah wahda anjaza wa'dah wa nasara

'abdah, wa hazamal-ahzaaba wahdah.) "There is no god but Allaah, the One who has no partner; sovereignty and praise are His and He has full power over everything. The is not god but Allaah, the One; He has fulfilled His promise (by subduing the whole of Arabia to Islaam), helped his servant and defeated the forces of disbelief by Himself."

He recited these words three times with a prayer in between. Then he descended Safaa, walked towards Marwah and repeated on Marwah the same prayers that he recited on Safaa.

When he came to Marwah for the last time, he addressed his companions from the top, saying, *"Had I known before now what I now know, I would not have brought the sacrificial animals with me and would have converted this **Tawaaf** and **Sa'yi** into that of 'Umrah and I would have taken off **Ihraam** after the performance of 'Umrah. However, those of your who have not brought the sacrificial offering along with them may regard this Tawaaf and Sa'yi as that of '**Umrah** and take off their **Ihraam**."* Hearing this, Suraqah ibn Maalik stood up and asked "O Messenger of Allaah! Is this command meant for this year only, or is it for the future as well?" The Prophet (ﷺ) intertwined the fingers of his two hands and said, *"Umrah and Hajj have been combined like this not only for this year, but forever!"*

When 'Alee arrived from Yeman with more sacrificial animals for the Prophet (ﷺ) and noticed that his wife Fatimah had set aside her *Ihraam*, put on colored clothes and applied antimony, he expressed his displeasure over this. But she told him that her father, the Prophet (ﷺ) himself, had allowed her to take off *Ihraam*.

The Prophet (ﷺ) turned to 'Alee and asked, *"What was your intention while putting on Ihraam?"* (That is, did you have the intention of performing Hajj only, or Hajj and 'Umrah both?) 'Alee replied that he had said, "O Allaah! My intention is the same as Your Prophet's" The Prophet (ﷺ) then said, *"Since I have brought the sacrificial offering along with me, I cannot take off Ihraam, and as your intention was the same as mine, you also cannot."*

Jaabir continued, "The total number of camels brought by the Prophet (ﷺ) and 'Alee as a sacrificial offering was 100. All the *Sahaabah* (companions of the Prophet) who had come without sacrificial animals took off their *Ihraam* garments and got their hair trimmed, while those who had brought sacrificial offerings with them remained in *Ihraam*. When the Day of *Tarweeyah* (i.e. 8th of *Thul-Hijjah*) came, the people started moving towards Minaa, and those who had taken off their *Ihraam* of 'Umrah resumed their *Ihraam* for *Hajj*. The Prophet (ﷺ) rode on his she-camel Qaswaa to Minaa, where he led all of the five prayers from *Thuhr* to *Fajr*. He then waited until sunrise and left for 'Arafah, where he ordered a tent pitched at Namirah. The Quraysh were sure that he would halt at Mash'ar al-Haraam, as had been the custom among them in the days of ignorance, but the Prophet (ﷺ) crossed the limits of Mash'ar al-Haraam, entered the bounds of 'Arafah and stayed in the tent that had been pitched for him at Namirah.

When the sun began to incline to the west, he ordered that Qaswaa should be saddled for him, and he rode to the bottom of the valley of 'Uranah where he sat on his camel and addressed the people saying,

"O People! Shedding of blood and seizing the properties of others in unlawful ways are forbidden on this day, in this month, in this city. Note well that all customs and practices of the days of ignorance are trampled under my feet; the blood feuds of the past are abolished, and first of all, I give up our family's claim as regards the son of Rabee'ah ibn al-Haarith ibn 'Abdul-Muttalib, who was being suckled by Banoo Sa'd when he was killed by Banoo Huthayl. Abolished also are all the claims of interest (Ribaa) of the past, and first of all I give up the claims in this respect of my uncle, 'Abbaas ibn 'Abdul-Muttalib.

"O People! Fear Allaah with regard to the right of your women. You have married them in Allaah's name and they have become lawful to you only by His law. Your special right on them is that they should not entertain anyone whom you dislike in your home, but if they commit an error in this regard, you may punish them lightly. The women's special right on you is that you should clothe and feed them generously according to your means.

"O People! If you hold fast to what I am leaving behind for you, and follow its teachings, you will never go astray. It is the Book of Allaah.

"O People! Each Muslim is a brother to every other Muslim, and all Muslims are brothers of one another. Therefore, the property of one is unlawful for the other unless given willingly, so do not be unjust to one another.

"On the Day of Resurrection, when you will be asked (about whether I have conveyed fully Allaah's message or not), what will you say?" The congregation spoke out with one voice, " We bear witness that you have conveyed to us the whole Divine Guidance in the best way possible and given us the best advice."

At this the Prophet (ﷺ) raised his forefinger towards the sky and then pointing to the congregation said thrice, *"O Allaah! May You also be a witness! I have conveyed Your Message and Your Commands to your people, as has been confirmed by them."*

Bilaal called the *Athaan* and pronounced the *Iqaamah* and the Prophet (ﷺ) lead the *Thuhr* prayer; Bilaal once again pronounced the *Iqaamah* and the Prophet (ﷺ) led the *'Asr* prayer. After performing the *Thuhr* and *'Asr* prayers together, the Prophet (ﷺ) rode to the plain of 'Arafaat and stopped there. He turned the back of his camel towards the big rocks and the front towards the multitude of people who had gathered there. He remained seated on the camel facing the *Qiblah* until the sun set and the yellowness of evening was gone. Then he set off for Muzdalifah with Usaamah ibn Zayd seated behind him on the camel.

When we reached Muzdalifah, he led the *Maghrib* and *'Eshaa'* prayers together with one *Athaan* and two *Iqaamahs* and nothing else between them. After this, he lay down for rest until it was dawn. He then led the *Fajr* prayer with one *Athaan* and an *Iqaamah*, and rode to Mash'ar al-Haraam where he stood facing the *Qiblah* and declaring Allaah's Greatness, His Oneness and His Glory for quite some time. When the daylight spread, he left for Minaa a little before sunrise with Fadl ibn 'Abbaas behind him on his camel. When he came to the bottom of the Valley of Muhassir, he urged his she-camel to go a bit faster. He then followed the middle path to the largest *Jamrah*, which was near a tree, and threw seven pebbles at it, saying *Allaahu Akbar* each time he threw. These were small pebbles, which he threw from the valley side. After this, he went to the place of sacrifice and slaughtered 63 camels with his own hand. The rest were slaughtered by 'Alee, whom he had taken as a partner in his sacrificial offerings. Then he ordered that a piece of flesh from each camel should be taken and cooked. After it was ready, he and 'Alee ate some of the meat and drank some of the soup. Then the Prophet (ﷺ) mounted his she-camel and left for the House of Allaah (to make *Tawaaf al-Efaadah*). He led the *Thuhr* prayer at Makkah and then approached the people of his clan (Banoo 'Abdul-Muttalib), who were drawing *Zamzam* water for the people to drink. He also asked them for water, saying, '*If I had not feared that the people, in their eagerness to follow me, would have forcibly taken this service of supplying water from you, I would have also drawn its waters along with you.*' They gave him a bucketful of water from which he drank."[181]

THE DAY BY DAY RITES OF HAJJ

Day One: The 8th Day of Thul-Hijjah

On the eighth day the pilgrim should put on his *Ihraam* and head out of Makkah to Minaa. He spends the whole day and night in Minaa involved in prayer, preparing himself to set out to 'Arafaat. He prays *Thuhr* and *'Asr* shortened two *Rak'ahs* units each, *Maghrib* three *Rak'ahs* and *'Eshaa'* shortened to two *Rak'ahs*.

Day Two: The 9th Day of Thul-Hijjah

This day is known as *Yawm 'Arafah*. After praying *Salaatul-Fajr* in Minaa, the pilgrim waits until just after sunrise, then he heads out of Minaa to the Plain of 'Arafah, which he should enter around noon.

In 'Arafah, he prays *Salaatuth-Thuhr* and *Salaatul- 'Asr* joined and shortened. He should then wait in 'Arafah until just after sunset, then set out to Muzdalifah (an area between 'Arafah and Minaa). There he should pray *Maghrib* and *'Eshaa'* together with *'Eshaa'* shortened, then spend the rest of the night in prayer and sleep.

---

[181] Collected by Muslim (*Sahih Muslim* (English Trans.), vol.2, pp.611-617, no.2803).

Day Three: The 10th Day of Thul-Hijjah

This day is known as 'Eid al-Ad-haa. The pilgrim should pray *Salaatul-Fajr* in Muzdalifah, then leave Muzdalifah for Minaa shortly before sunrise. In Minaa he collects seven small stones and heads for the largest *Jamrah*. As he throws each stone at the *Jamrah*, he should say *Allaahu Akbar*. On completion of the rites of stoning, he should clip or shave his head and take off his *Ihraam*.

He should then go to the place where animals are kept and slaughter an animal if he is making a *Hajj Qiraan* or *Hajj Tamattu'*. After that he goes to Makkah and makes seven circuits of the *Ka'bah*, known as *Tawaaf al-Efaadah*, then returns to Minaa and spends the rest of the night there.

Day Four: The 11th Day of Thul-Hijjah

On this day he should pray *Fajr* in Minaa and wait until after *Thuhr*, then he should head for the three *Jamrahs*. On the way there, he collects enough pebbles with which to stone all three of them. He should start with *Jamratul-Oolaa*, then *al-Wastaa* and *al-'Aqabah*.

Day Five: The 12th Day of Thul-Hijjah

He does as he did on the 11th and, on the completion of the stoning, he is allowed to return home. Before leaving the vicinity of Makkah, the pilgrim should perform the farewell *Tawaaf*, known as *Tawaaf al-Widaa'*.

Day Six: The 13th Day of Thul-Hijjah

It is recommended that the pilgrim stay for the 13th and do exactly as he did on the 11th and 12th. After completing the stoning, he should then perform the farewell *Tawaaf* of the *Ka'bah* before leaving Makkah.

QUESTIONS

1. Islamically, *Hajj* means
    (a) to set out on a journey for a place.
    (b) to perform *'Umrah* in a state of *Ihraam* during the months of *Hajj*.
    (c) the pilgrimage to Madeenah in a state of *Ihraam* during the month of *Hajj* and the performance of certain religious rites.
    (d) the journey to Makkah in a state and performance of set religious rites there.
    (e) pilgrimage to the *Ka'bah* and doing special rites in the months of *Hajj*.

2. *Hajj* is only compulsory if one is a
    (a) sane Muslim male past the age of puberty.
    (b) Muslim male who has reached puberty and is physically fit.
    (c) sane male or female past puberty and physically and monetarily able to make the journey.
    (d) Muslim of sound mind and body having sufficient money to make the trip.
    (e) none of the above.

3. The three types of *Hajj* are
    (a) *Hajj Ifraad*, *Hajj Qiraan* and *Hajj Tawaaf*.
    (b) *Hajj Widaa'*, *Hajj Ifraad* and *Hajj Qiraan*.
    (c) *Hajj Qiraan*, *Hajj Tamattu'* and *Hajj Arafah*.
    (d) *Hajj Tamattu'*, *Hajj Efaadah* and *Hajj Qiraan*.
    (e) *Hajj Ifraad*, *Hajj Tamattu'* and *Hajj Qiraan*.

4. A correct description of one type of *Hajj* is
    (a) *Hajj Qiraan* consists of *Hajj* with *'Umrah*, but not sacrifice.
    (b) *Hajj* without *'Umrah* and sacrifice, known as *Hajj 'Efaadah*.
    (c) *'Umrah* along with Hajj and a sacrifice, known as *Hajj Tawaaf*.
    (d) *Hajj Ifraad* is *Hajj* without *'Umrah* and without going to *'Arafah*.
    (e) *Hajj* with *'Umrah* and a sacrifice is called *Hajj Tamattu'*.

5. The pilgrim should go to 'Arafah on the
   (a) 9th day of _Thul-Qa'dah_.
   (b) 8th day of _Thul-Hijjah_.
   (c) 9th day of _Thul-Hijjah_.
   (d) 10 th day of _Thul-Hijjah_.
   (e) 10 th day of _Thul-Qa'dah_.

6. On the 10th day of _Thul-Hijjah_, the pilgrim should
   (a) go to Muzdalifah after sunset.
   (b) stone the three _Jamaraat_ after _Thuhr_.
   (c) go to Makkah and make _Tawaaf al-Efaadah_.
   (d) shave his hair in the plain of 'Arafaat.
   (e) perform the farewell _Tawaaf_, known as _Tawaaf al-Widaa'_.

7. The main difference between the rites of the 12th day and those of the 13th is
   (a) the stoning which must be done before _Thuhr_ on the 12 th and after _Thuhr_ on the 13th.
   (b) that those of the 12th are compulsory, while those of the 13 the are optional.
   (c) the farewell _Tawaaf_, which must be made on the 12th if one is staying on until the 13th.
   (d) that on the 12th only the largest _Jamrah_ is stoned, while on the 13th all three are to be stoned.
   (e) that the rites of the 12th are optional, while those of the 13th are compulsory.

193